GHOST TOWNS
and Other Historical Sites
of the
BLACK HILLS

Cover photo: Old Business District of St. Onge.

THE
DONNING COMPANY
PUBLISHERS

GHOST TOWNS
and Other Historical Sites
of the
BLACK HILLS

by Bruce A. Raisch

An abandoned church in the Inyan Kara Valley, Wyoming.

The Donning Company Publishers
184 Business Park Drive, Suite 206
Virginia Beach, VA 23462–6533

Steve Mull, General Manager
Barbara Buchanan, Office Manager
Jamie R. Watson, Editor
Amanda D. Guilmain, Graphic Designer
Amy Thomann, Imaging Artist
Scott Rule, Director of Marketing
Stephanie Linneman, Marketing Coordinator

Carey Southwell, Project Director

Library of Congress Cataloging-in-Publication Data

Raisch, Bruce A., 1956-
  Ghost towns and other historical sites of the Black Hills / by Bruce
A. Raisch.
      p. cm.
  Includes bibliographical references.
  ISBN-13: 978-1-57864-351-6 (alk. paper)
  ISBN-10: 1-57864-351-1 (alk. paper)
 1. Ghost towns--Black Hills Region (S.D. and Wyo.) 2. Ghost
towns--Black Hills Region (S.D. and Wyo.)--Pictorial works. 3. Black
Hills Region (S.D. and Wyo.)--History. 4. Black Hills Region (S.D.
and Wyo.)--History--Pictorial works. I. Title.
  F657.B6R3 2006
  978.3'9--dc22
                                        2005037801
Printed in the United States of America by Walsworth Publishing
Company, Marceline, MO.

DEDICATION

It is with great pride that I dedicate this book to my eldest niece,
Lauren. When she enlisted in the Army National Guard at age
eighteen, not only did she join my old unit, the First Missouri,
she also became the fourth generation of my family to serve at the
historic Jefferson Barracks.

Duty, Honor, Country are much more than just three words.

ACKNOWLEDGMENTS

While researching this book, I had the opportunity to meet and talk with many people. They answered questions, gave directions and sometimes even gave geology lessons. Whether by phone, mail, or while on the road, they appeared for just a moment in my life but have enriched it forever. They are clerks, gas station attendants, small-town mayors, operators, librarians, prospectors, storekeepers, and waitresses. I came as a stranger but they treated me as a friend.

Places like Accidental Oil and Four Mile were fun and informative. The staff was cheerful and eager to please. The sites are family-friendly, family-owned, and family-operated. When you meet a member of the staff, there is a good chance he or she is a member of that family.

Thanks to individuals such as Steve Baldwin, executive director of the Black Hills Park and Forest Association. He reviewed the text, helped with research and has been very supportive of this project. Many people gladly shared information about their past or present communities. Thanks to Phyllis Miller, a fourteen-year resident of Igloo, who not only provided many details, but also invited me to Igloo's annual reunion.

Staff at Custer State Park, Pactola Lake Visitor Center, and the Black Hills National Forest headquarters at Custer, South Dakota, were all of great assistance on occasions too numerous to list. A special thanks goes to Sharon McQuillen at the USDA Forest Service. The USDA Forest Service sells a map of the Black Hills that was used for both research and navigation. I am grateful for the consistently professional and helpful manner of the western states' tourism and transportation departments. A special thanks also goes to all the U.S. Postal Service personnel who provided a great deal of information, always with a smile.

To Patricia Cracchiola, to whom I often refer as "my staff," must go more than just a "thanks," but the recognition that she is an important part of this book.

THE ROAD
to welcome

A ghost town is a mere shadow of its former self. What began as a curiosity about them became a passion. Along the way, a process was born. This section describes my method of finding and choosing which locations to physically explore.

I do a bit of everything when researching to determine the locations. First, with the appropriate state highway map in hand, I go to the library. Here, I grab books on the state and ghost towns, request books if they are not in-house, and then check the Internet. Many states are listed on several websites. Then I start searching for other ghost towns missed by everyone else.

I end up giving 411 a lot of business. I obtain telephone numbers for city hall, the chamber of commerce, museums, parks departments, the post office, tourist businesses, and visitor centers for the town in question or other towns in the same area. Of course, I do not limit

This is the actual road to the township of Welcome.

The author gets a geology lesson from a gold prospector who called himself, "Two Dollar Johnnie."

myself to 411. Each state has a fair number of government agencies such as tourism, transportation, and parks departments that are more than willing to provide mounds of information. The contacts I establish provide not only possible locations and history, but also additional contacts in a domino-like fashion.

One of the best ways to find old town locations is to look at old maps. Comparing dated highway maps with newer ones gives me a wealth of locations to check.

After conducting all possible research via books, the Internet, mail, maps, and phone, I take the next logical step and visit the sites in person. I am not satisfied about the site until my size-12D boots have personally walked one of the streets of the old town. I take notes and photos and interview anyone with knowledge of the local history. A handheld tape recorder is a great asset in such fieldwork. I like to know what to look for and what I am looking at. If you do not know what a tailings pile is, you will not know when you are standing on one. Remember, take only photos, leave only footprints.

After a trip to the research area, I conduct follow-up interviews and review my information. Together, the notes, tapes, and photos create a mosaic of history, much like a jigsaw puzzle that I then reassemble.

"The Road to Welcome" refers to both an actual location and the manner in which you should strive to be received. Besides being the right thing to do, behaving politely will greatly further field research results. Do not litter, trespass, leave off-road tire tread marks, or collect souvenirs that are not for sale. Close any gate you open. Do not take an individual's photo without permission. Adhere to the local parking and traffic regulations. Then smile, say "hello," and give a firm handshake. I do this on any trip.

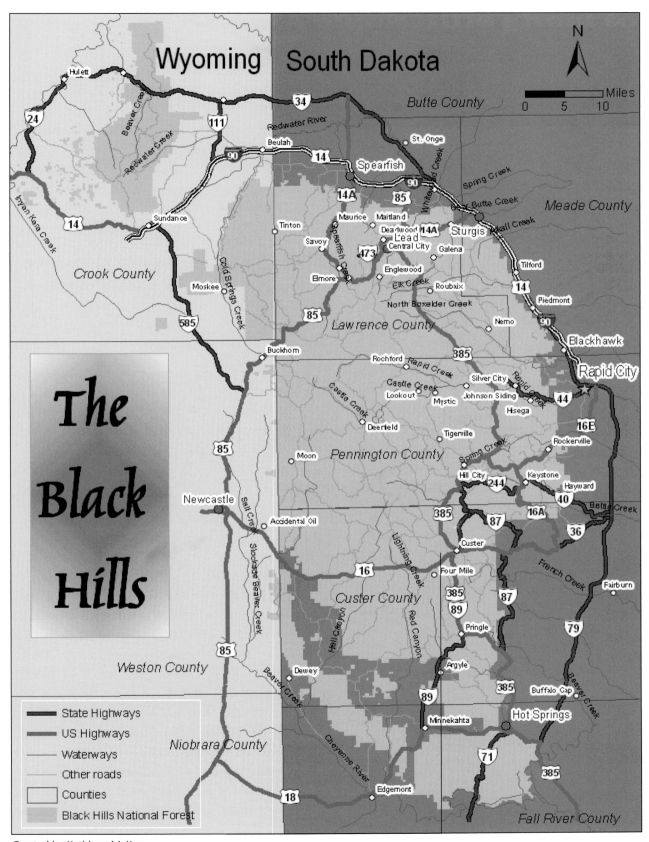

The Black Hills

HISTORY

of the black hills boom

The history of the Black Hills revolves around natural resources. People were drawn to the region because of natural resources; they fought over them as well. This historical summary begins with the western migration era in which so many of the region's ghost towns were born.

Gold- and land-hungry white settlers drove out the Sioux. Before ringing your hands in politically correct guilt, note that history shows that the Sioux had previously taken the land from the Crow and Cheyenne Indians in the 1770s for its game, timber, and hunting grounds. The archeological evidence shows that, before that, the Crow had evicted another group for the same reasons. The white man wanted the land for its furs, timber, summer grazing grounds, and the rumor of gold.

Numerous abandoned mines dot the Black Hills. There are many hazards, from rattlesnakes to pitfalls to poisonous gases. Do not enter!

Driving around the Black Hills can be challenging and difficult. This is one of three tunnels on the Needles Highway.

A small French expedition in 1743 was the first reported visit by white men to the Black Hills. This group consisted of brothers Francois and Louis Verendrye. Their trip was forgotten in time, but their adventures were rediscovered in 1913. Meriwether Lewis, William Clark, and the Corps of Discovery were the next white men to spot the Black Hills. The journals mention and refer to the region as the "Black Mountains." However, Lewis and Clark did not explore the region. Another known to see the Hills was William Price Hunt in 1811. He and a few others traveled the northern fringe of the Hills along the Belle Fourche River.

A party of fur trappers, led by the renowned Jedediah Smith, was the first group of white men known to explore the Black Hills. Smith was almost mauled to death by a grizzly bear along French Creek during this time. Probably about twelve men made the October 1823 trip. As a result, two fur trading posts were set up on the Hills' edge by 1828.

Over the next couple of decades, several mapping and hunting expeditions combed the Hills. But it was the rumor of gold that forced them open to settlement. Frontier army posts and stagecoach stations were there before the gold rush. Various sources give the year of the first discovery of the ore as being anywhere from 1804 to 1865, but it was the Custer expedition of 1874 that started the stampede.

By 1874, most American Indians were on a reservation, but not the Sioux. In 1868, the Black Hills had been ceded to them through the Treaty of Fort Laramie. This ten-million-acre prairie oasis was spiritually important to them. It also mattered to their survival as a hunting tribe. They would not let it go without a fight. George Custer, a colonel in the U.S. Army at the time, meant to give them one. The Sioux would make their last stand in the Black Hills. Custer would make his on Little Bighorn. They would both lose.

Bighorn sheep are not native to the Black Hills but were introduced to the area. Like a lot of wildlife, they are great to photograph. But as the author found out in Wyoming, they can be dangerous. Do not feed or approach.

Frequent skirmishes were breaking out with the Sioux over railroad construction in Wyoming, gold prospectors trespassing in the Black Hills, and the increasingly large number of white settlers pushing west. Often the Seventh Cavalry and its leader, "Yellow Hair," as the Sioux called Custer, were called to act as escorts or counterattack the Indian raids.

In response to these raids, the U.S. government ordered a military expedition to the heart of the Black Hills. The construction of a fort was necessary to control the "Indian problem." Custer was chosen to lead this mission. After several delays, the expedition left Fort Lincoln, Nebraska, on July 2, 1874. It included 110 wagons, more than 660 mules, 1,000 cavalry horses, 300 head of cattle, 3 Gatling guns, and artillery. More than one thousand men were part of the expedition, including civilian interpreters, teamsters, blacksmiths, herders, Indian guides, and others. This

Just as in Yellowstone, buffalo are allowed to roam free in Custer State Park. They are big, beautiful, and extremely dangerous.

force was not meant to surprise anyone. It was supposed to be large enough so that the Indians would not want to bother with it. Custer, in his style, took about as many reporters as he did scientists on the trip. The sixteen-member military band was larger than the group of reporters and scientists combined.

Soon the group discovered gold on French Creek. The news was made public on August 12, 1874, even before Custer returned to Fort Lincoln on August 30. The rush was on. By December 1874, another party had reached French Creek. General Phillip Sheridan immediately issued orders to all area commanders to stop the stampede, but the effort failed. After about one year, it was decided to remove the Indians from the area instead.

Other expeditions did much to open the Hills to settlement. The Jenney Expedition in 1875 was among them. The expedition was a scientific exploration and was named for the professor who led the group.

One expedition that was meant to stop settlement here had the opposite effect. General George A. Crook led troops into the Hills to drive miners out, but other prospectors followed in his tracks. Three early gold-mining camps were named Camp Crook because General Crook's force had, at one time, rested at those sites. Miners following his party rested at the same spots and would often discover placer gold. These miners immediately set up shop.

The gold rush caused the accidental discovery of silver in the area. Prospectors were almost as happy with this as with the gold. Often, when you find silver, you find lead. The Hills were no exception. These discoveries caused additional mining booms. Later, there would be rushes for coal, tin, and oil. With these industries came a boom-and-bust business cycle.

The history of the Black Hills railroad industry is closely tied to the mining industry. Together, the industries caused the creation of the timber industry in the region. Those three industries combined gave birth to the majority of towns, including ghost towns, in these Hills.

The Homestake Mining Company built the first narrow-gauge railroad in the Hills in 1881 at Lead. It was built to haul mining supplies and passengers from Lead to several mining camps on higher ground. The first railroad to bring supplies into the Hills was a standard gauge line that reached Buffalo Gap in 1885. By 1886, the line was extended to Rapid City.

Before railroads, stagecoaches and freight wagon companies provided major public transportation. These companies built rough roads and established stage stations on them at five- to ten-mile intervals. The first freight roads and stage stations were established in the Black Hills in 1876. Often the stations became forts, trading posts, or towns. Railroads would later follow some of the roads when tracks were laid. Many times, railway section towns were built on the previous sites of the stage stations. Only faint traces of the roads or stage stations remain today.

A whole cast of colorful characters from western folklore are threaded within the history of the sleepy communities, including Calamity Jane and Wild Bill Hickok. Numerous Black Hills towns, past and present, lay claim to a visit by one or both of them. Wild Bill was shot dead in Deadwood during a card game in 1876. His final poker hand was two pairs—aces and eights, now known as the "dead man's hand."

Calamity Jane, who at one time worked as a prostitute, passed herself off as a man and got a job as a teamster. A photo from the time shows her dressed like a man and quite homely. During her

Hidden in the underbrush, an old tractor and an even older cabin attest to busier times in Cascade, South Dakota.

short life, Calamity Jane had frequently claimed a romance with Wild Bill, a claim he had always denied. She died in Terry, South Dakota, near Deadwood, on August 1, 1903. What Calamity Jane could not have in life, she obtained in death. As she requested, she was buried next to Hickok in Deadwood's Boothill. Hollywood has linked the two for eternity.

Depending on the source, the Black Hills gold rush is claimed to have produced between six hundred and one thousand towns. In the 1950s, there were numerous ghost towns in the

Black Hills. Most were from this boom period. As recently as the late 1970s, there were a large number of towns, some with huge mills standing by for operations. There are but a fraction of them left. Most of what is left today is in bad shape. Some of the best that remain, such as Tinton and Trojan, are in danger of being obliterated by current mining operations. Time and tourists are taking care of the rest. However, tourism has also led to the reconstruction of such sites as Four Mile and Rockerville and the partial preservation of others like Castleton, Mystic, and Rochford.

I read as many books as I could about Black Hills ghost towns. By far, the best one was *Black Hills Ghost Towns* by Watson Parker and Hugh K. Lambert. All of the books were rather dated, the newest being from 1979. My book picks up where some of the better, but dated, ones left off.

BLACK HILLS

ghost towns and other
historical sites

SOUTH DAKOTA SITES VISITED

Addie Camp
Cascade
Castleton
Crook City
Four Mile
Galena
Lookout
Maitland
Moon
Myersville
Mystic
Pringle
Redfern
Rochford
Rockerville
Roubaix
Spokane
Teddy Bear
Tigerville
Trojan

SITES NOT VISITED

Alta
Annie Creek
Astoria
Balmoral
Bear Gulch
Canyon City
Carbonate
Englewood
Preston
Silver City
Victoria

WYOMING SITES VISITED

Cambria (Coal Mine)
Cambria (Salt Mine)
Inyan Kara
Mineral Hill
Moskee
Tinton
Tubb Town/Field City
Welcome

RAILROAD GHOST TOWNS OF SOUTH DAKOTA SITES VISITED

Ardmore
Buffalo Gap
Fairburn
Imlay
Oral
Provo
Rumford
St. Onge
Scenic

SITES NOT VISITED

Burdock
Conata
Creston
Dewey
Smithwick

OTHER HISTORICAL SITES

Accidental Oil
Anna Miller Museum
CCC Camps
Cambria Casino
Central City
Flag Mountain Overlook
Gordon Stockade
Harney Peak
Igloo
Oblivion
Pactola Lake Visitor Center
1880 Train

SOUTH DAKOTA

black hills ghost towns

ADDIE CAMP (Pennington County)

Addie Camp was founded in the 1880s as a mining town.
Throughout its history, it has also been known as Addie Spur,
Canadaville, and Kennedyville. It got these last two names from a
house that doubled as the town grocery store and bar. The names
came from the family that owned it at one time. The house remains
today and is occupied. The town is located 2 1/2 miles east of Hill
City, on the old Hill City–Keystone road, a two-lane blacktop also
known as County Road 323.

The mining operation was different from most mines. Instead of
being owned by U.S. citizens, it was owned and operated by an
English company called the Harney Peak Tin Mining, Milling and
Manufacturing Company.

Mount Rushmore National Memorial is one of the most breathtaking sites in the
Black Hills.

This was the Kennedy House, which once doubled as the town's grocery store and bar.

It was also different for the Black Hills at that time because it mined tin instead of gold. Here cassiterite ore from deposits near Keystone and Hill City were processed. At Addie Mine, shafts were dug to the depth of eight hundred feet. Very little tin was found.

Addie Camp got a boost when it became a railroad stop in February 1900. The line had been extended to Keystone, and Addie Camp had acquired a station with a platform. Today the 1880 tourist train passes through the town using this same route.

The Chicago, Burlington and Quincy Railroad built a spur from Hill City to Addie Camp in the early 1890s to tap the mining and timber hauling business. A half-mile railroad spur was connected to Addie Mine in December 1892 to haul tin ore out to the mill east of Hill City. Like so many operating mines in the West, this one failed to make a profit. The tracks for the railroad spur were ripped up in

1917. Currently, the spur is on private property. At this time, the town became a farming community.

Today all that remains are some homes, mostly abandoned, scattered over a fairly sizable area. Mine ruins are in a farmer's pasture. One of the occupied homes was the old saloon. Please be considerate; there are still a few residents here. Abandoned mines, such as the Goldenville, Good Luck Tungsten Mine, and the Grisly Bear, are in the general area. The Good Luck mine is easily visible from either County Road 323 or the 1880 Train route. Most of the tungsten mined here was done during the two World Wars and was used to harden steel.

ALTA (Pennington)
SITE NOT VISITED

Alta is Myersville's twin sister. It was named after the Alta Lodi Mining Company and its old mine. The community was started before 1878 and was also called Alta Mine. By 1878, a small population of about twenty lived around the Alta mine. It grew from there and became a small town.

In 1883, Alta Lodi Mining Company probably built their forty-stamp mill here instead of in Myersville proper. The mill and the mine

Left: Some of the old original Addie Camp cabins, like this one, are still used.

Top: Telegraph poles along the old Burlington Railroad line still mark the way to Addie Camp.

Bottom: Numerous structures at Addie Camp lie in ruins. This one appeared to be larger than a typical miner's shack.

failed, so Alta folded up. Myersville hung on for a while longer. The mill was moved to Lookout and was expanded to a fifty-stamper. The area was reworked by James Cochran from 1892 until 1917. The whole area was prospected or worked on and off through 1936, but Alta's population was already gone. For additional information, see Myersville in this section.

When visiting Myersville, I lacked prior knowledge of Alta; therefore, I did not search the area for any of its remains. If there are any of Alta, it was not obvious. Alta should lie directly east of Myersville, across a pasture and slightly within the wood line. The Alta mine should also be here. The people of Alta probably used the Myersville cemetery for their deceased.

ANNIE CREEK (Lawrence)
SITE NOT VISITED

This was a gold-mining camp, located near Trojan, in the northern Black Hills. It was originally called Reliance after the mine born at the same time. The site is in a wooded valley along the banks of Annie Creek. Gold was produced here until at least 1916. Books, websites, and National Forest maps show many buildings, but recent mining in the area has wiped out much of the past in this district. Between mining and other development, most of the towns like Preston, Terry, and Trojan had recently succumbed to man.

Maps show two roads into Annie Creek. I chose the road from Trojan, but the route was barred due to current open-pit mining operations. The other option is to take 14A to the National Forest road that parallels Annie Creek and then head north.

Annie Creek is reportedly located 1 1/2 miles southwest of Trojan and two miles northeast of Elmore.

ASTORIA (Lawrence)
SITE NOT VISITED

A gold-mining camp popped up here in 1887. The Golden Reward Gold Mining Company operated a mill and smelter. Ore was processed from their own mine and from the hundreds of small operations dotting the Ruby Basin and Bald Mountain mining districts. Ore was delivered to the mill by pack animal, wagons, and narrow- and standard-gauge trains. The mill operated through at least 1918. It was reportedly a pioneer in the use of natural gas for smelting.

Several sources claim there are remains here. They state the location is west of U.S. Highway 85 and approximately 2 1/2 miles southwest of Lead. It is possible that time has overtaken these sources. Topographic maps and local directions would be required.

Avenues such as Castle Creek Road make for a dream of a drive in good weather, but in snow or rain, these roads can turn into nightmares!

BALMORAL (Lawrence)
SITE NOT VISITED

This was one of several settlements that sprang up around Ragged Top Mountain. Silicified gold ore was discovered around the area at a shallow depth in 1897.

By 1900, Balmoral had grown into a core business district at a crossroads with a small number of outlying homes. Other towns that had supposedly been in the area were Cyanide, Dacy, Preston, and Victoria. In fact, Preston was only a quarter mile away; numerous sources still confuse the two locations. One rather dated U.S. Geological Survey map shows Cyanide as a latter-day name for Balmoral. Cyanide did exist as a town; it had its own school and post office, circa 1915. That it is a latter-day name for Balmoral is possible but unlikely. The issue of the exact number and names of towns in this former mining district is open to debate.

Remains are said to be a few homes, scattered sheds, and a reportedly well-preserved Ragged Top School. These claims are rather dated (they are from the 1970s). Still, some sources place the Top School in Preston. In their book, even Parker and Lambert are confused as to which location the school belongs.

The whole location may have disappeared due to a large open-pit mining operation being conducted by Wharf Mining Company.

BEAR GULCH (Lawrence)
SITE NOT VISITED

Going back to at least 1877, this was one of the first placer gold camps, or any other kind of settlement for that matter, in the Negro Hill mining district. By 1880, it had boomed to a population of more than one thousand. The town lasted longer than the gold boom

The road network in the Black Hills is extensive. It can be a challenge to drive because no two maps of the area are alike, and numerous routes are not shown on any maps at all.

Livestock are a hazard on the roads even more frequently than wildlife.

only by jumping on the tin boom. Even with this switch, Bear Gulch experienced a sharp and rapid decline. By 1887, the town had a small number of tin mines, quartz mills, two sawmills, a tin smelter, and a post office but only two hundred residents. As the tin boom played out, so did Bear Gulch. The town had only one hundred residents by 1900, and the decline continued until it hit zero.

Websites and books claim the town site of Bear Gulch is a half-mile northeast of Tinton. Maps show neither town site nor mine there. The actual gulch—after which the town was named and in which the town was located—is shown to be about three miles due north of Tinton. Remains are unknown to me but would be stretched out for some distance along the creek that runs through the gulch. Written sources claim you can drive right to the site; maps show no roads into Bear Gulch and that a hike would be required. The written sources are usually rather dated and Black Hills maps are notorious for omissions and inaccuracies. Photos from the 1970s show well-preserved log cabins that appear to have been occupied in the recent past. Various sources claim remains here, but these claims are unconfirmed.

CANYON CITY (Pennington)
SITE NOT VISITED

The site of Canyon City rests along Rapid Creek between Mystic and Silver City. This was a placer mining camp, mine mill, and small transportation center for the Black Hills and Western Railroad. Its peak population is estimated to have been around four hundred. Several maps and reference sources report a few remains here, but this cannot be confirmed because the information is rather dated. The abandoned railbed of the Black Hills and Western Railway should still run through the site.

To reach this location, you must hike in. The easiest way is from the north. Take the Kelly Gulch Road (National Forest Road 742) to its end and you should see the trailhead. Another trail runs east-west through the Rapid and Slate Creek basins, but this is a much longer hike. The Canyon City location is marked on the Black Hills National Forest map.

CARBONATE (Lawrence)
SITE NOT VISITED

Carbonate was founded about 1881 as an apple farm. As such, it was a very small community. When the apple farm's owner, James Ridpath, staked out a silver mine, a town started to grow. His mine was called the West Virginia and so was the town for a short while. The name was quickly shortened to Virginia. It then changed to Carbonate Camp and, finally, Carbonate. By 1885, it had become a fairly sizable town.

At its peak, it is claimed that a population between two and three thousand lived here. There were stores, saloons, gambling halls, boardinghouses, a large hotel, a bank, post office, and at least one church. A smelter was built just east of town in 1887.

There were six mines here, the most important being Iron Hill. It was worked from at least 1885 until some time in the 1930s. It was the last mine to close here. Most of the others had closed between 1891 and 1904. In 1901, Iron Hill's mine dump was profitably reworked for 91 tons of lead and 18,511 ounces of silver. The town died a slow death. By 1891 a number of mines had played out, and the price of silver had plunged.

Carbonate's smelter used a pyrite flick that was heavy with arsenic. The fumes from its use killed much of the vegetation and all the cats in town. In 1889, an epidemic of black diphtheria hit, and a wave of people fled. For years afterward, their abandoned houses were still fearfully marked "Keep Out - Black Diphtheria."

The large Hugginson Hotel was torn down in 1900 to supply lumber for the nearby Cleopatra Mill and Mine, which was west of Carbonate, in the valley of what was then called Squaw Creek, now Coolidge Creek. Also here was the small mining camp named Squaw Creek.

Around 1910, there were some efforts to rework the tailings in Carbonate. Different attempts at production from Iron Hill continued until the 1930s. In 1939, the town's last inhabitant died.

This location is shown by name on the Black Hills National Forest map. Books and maps claim remains here, but all sources were rather dated. Some state that the old apple orchards are still there. If there were any remains, they would be scattered over a wide area and easy to confuse with adjacent sites such as Squaw Creek.

There are several ways into Carbonate. None should be easy. The location is northwest of Maitland and east of Spearfish Canyon. You will need a topographic map and the appropriate navigation skills. Best to try it in the summer because of road and trail conditions.

CASCADE (Fall River)
Cascade was born in 1888 as a resort town; it was known as Cascade

During Cascade's boom period, this was the W. Allen Bank. Today, it is a modernized and rehabbed private residence.

This Victorian-style house was the residence of the town's banker.

Springs. It is located in the Alabough Canyon, nine miles south of Hot Springs and two miles north of Cascade Falls on State Highway 71. The resort itself was located near a warm mineral spring called Cascade Spring, hence the town's name. The spring never freezes. It flows at a rate of about two thousand gallons of warm water a minute.

At this time, the railroad was building a route northward towards Hot Springs. It was hoped the railroad would pass through and stop at this resort town. Between the railroad and the resort, boomers had high hopes for Cascade.

A large four-story, one hundred–room hotel that has been described as ornate was built around the time the town was founded. It was constructed of local sandstone, just like the W. Allen Bank in town. It had high ceilings, towering chimneys, and rows of tall, narrow windows. Also in town was the two-story frame Cascade Club with its extended bowling alley for entertainment. The club had a second-story entrance for the snow season. A fair number of the town's buildings had this same feature. Altogether, thirty-six city blocks, including a business district, were laid out and partially constructed.

The town's boom did not last long. Developers got greedy and demanded too high a price for the right-of-way to the Burlington and Missouri River Railroad. Instead, the railroad took an alternate route and bypassed Cascade, as did time. This was a fairly common way for western towns to die. In an era before good roads, a town needed to be a port, on a river, or serviced by a train for it to boom. It was also common for developers to kill a town at birth by seeking too high a land price from the railroad. You'll see this all over again in the Wyoming ghost town of Tubb Town. By 1900, only twenty-five people remained in Cascade, and the only business left open was the post office.

Today there is even less here. The Parker and Lambert book is a great reference but rather dated about the description of remains. From their description, less than half the site remains.

For a long time, a section of the business block remained. It consisted of the W. Allen Bank, the general store, a bar, and the Cascade Club and bowling alley. The store, known as the Fargo store, had a brick façade, but this was stripped or fell away with time. The sides and rear were built solely of lumber. The Cascade Club was the major source of entertainment in town. All large buildings were set with tall, narrow windows. In the days before air conditioning, people were concerned with airflow for interior cooling purposes.

Today, all that remains of the business block is the bank. Even the remains of the Cascade Hotel have been picked clean. Only small piles of sandstone blocks dot the town site. Most of the stones were used to build a Catholic church and the Sister's Hospital in Hot Springs. Both of these buildings have been torn down, and most of

The building in the foreground was originally the livery stable.

the blocks are in storage at Hot Springs. A few of the blocks were used there in the construction of a local motel. The old bank was bought in the late 1970s, rehabbed and converted into a beautiful residence. The other buildings in the business section were all torn down for safety purposes and yard space.

The two-story frame house of Mr. Allen—the banker—still remains intact. The Victorian-style woodwork porches have recently been stripped away from here. The old livery stable remains. It too had been converted into a house but then abandoned again. Behind the bank, there is an old log cabin that was converted into a shed. Piles of sandstone, ruins of a wagon, holes from old foundations, and other debris are scattered about.

The whole site rests in a beautiful setting and is bisected by Cascade Creek.

CASTLETON (Pennington)

Castleton was started by gold placer miners in 1876. As such, it is one of the first communities of the Black Hills. Castle Creek, which bisected the town, was the source of the placer deposits. (General Custer named the creek in 1874 when he and his troops moved through the stream's headwaters.) Gold was first discovered farther west, in the valley, during 1875, and the stampede was on. In fact, at one time during the Black Hills gold rush, the Castle Creek valley was the most populated part of South Dakota.

A water flume project was started so that more gold deposits could be tapped. The flume had to be dug by hand in solid bedrock. About this time, the population probably peaked at about 250, and the town consisted of about fifty cabins, a number of saloons, a hotel, grocery store, and a jewelry shop. The flume did not carry enough water and lacked sufficient grade, so the project failed. The placer finds soon played out—in other words, they ran out. The remaining gold was in bedrock in the hills or in the creekbed under twenty-five feet of water, gravel, dirt, and their own tailings.

There is a small year-round population.

Remains of this historical site are scattered and sparse.

When the flume failed, most miners drifted to new digs. By 1880, four-fifths of the people were gone and their cabins abandoned. A few of the businesses hung on until the 1920s. Even during its peak, Castleton's residents supplemented their gold mining with ranching and farming to support themselves.

In the late 1880s, the town became a railroad construction center for the Burlington, which was building a line to Deadwood. Besides laying track, the crews here were building a small trestle, digging two tunnels, and cutting a number of embankments into the hills. These embankment cuts and the railroad bed are still visible in town today. In the early 1890s, it was virtually abandoned again. At this time, most of the town was homesteaded by Denny O'Brien.

Another attempt at gold mining took place in 1911 and continued through 1914. This time, with financing from the Evans family of Denver, Castle Creek was dredged. The large dredge was placed on a barge. It all ran by electricity. It scooped up the creek in front of it, washed the rock, and deposited the tailings behind itself. The operation failed because the creek bottom consisted of irregular bedrock. In 1915, the dredge was disassembled from the barge and

The weather-beaten wagon, rebuilt log cabin, and tin-roof shed all show the age of this community.

shipped to a buyer in John Day, Oregon. Today, the ribs of the barge sticking out of the earth are all that remains of the dredge.

Castleton had three booms but never grew to any size. When the railroad stopped running, the town just about dried up. Today, it claims nine residents, but I have my doubts. Most of the cabins here appear to be of the summer cottage variety. Tailings and dredge lines are common, and the Glory Hunter Mine is nearby.

Most of the old dredge line, with its tailings piles, has been bought up by the Glory Hunter Mine. The owners are sure they can find the gold everyone else has missed. The Glory Hunter Mine group is also operating at a site up Castle Creek that has been mined on and off since 1876. Here mining is done by hand. The ore is put in old painter's buckets and then hauled back to Castleton in a pickup truck. The old dredge pools make good swimming and fishing holes, but most, if not all, are on private property.

This location has the advantage of being able to offer a National Forest Campground nearby. The Castle Peak campground is about five miles up Castle Creek Road and makes a nice picnic stop or a place to camp for the evening after a day of Black Hills ghost-town hunting. In fair weather, the road is easily passable in a family vehicle.

There are a small number of hard rock mines in the hills around town. Some, including the Glory Hunter, still operate sporadically. Castleton is located in the heart of the Black Hills, but it is mostly on private property. For some unexplained reason, Castleton is not marked on National Forest maps, whereas the likes of diminutive Redfern is. Even though it is not marked on many maps, it is still easy to find. Just follow County Road 308 out of Hill City. The route to Castleton is scenic, well-marked, paved up to the first turn off, and only about twelve miles long. After 5.2 miles, you will come to a crossroads at Tigerville, another small ghost, and veer right. This is County Road 318 or National Forest Road 231. If the road numbering system appears confusing to you, don't worry; it is. Two miles north of Tigerville on this road is the minor site of Redfern. There is less here than at Tigerville.

An additional 2.7 miles north of Redfern brings you to the site of the Mystic CCC Camp F-1. The camp was in a pasture on the west side of the road and is marked by a roughly carved stone slab. The camp operated from June 29, 1933, to January 6, 1938, and housed about two hundred personnel.

Just 2.6 miles north of that, you will bump into Castleton. As far as remains, there is more here than you will notice at first glance. The gravel tailings in Castle Creek from the dredge operation are very noticeable. A small number of barns, cabins, shacks, and even old wagons dot the landscape. Most of these buildings have been occupied more than once. The majority of what is still standing is being used in one way or another. The population of Castleton, according to one of three signs in town, is nine. This probably increases in the summer because a few old cabins have been converted to summer cottages.

This is an old mill wheel that has been reconstructed by local residents.

A few rotten remains of timber from a barge on which the dredge sat are at the south end of the tailings. A paddlewheel used for waterpower rests upright in the creek. The old railroad cuts and embankments lay above and to the east of town. Operating on and off in the center of town is Glory Hunter Mine. There are the common sights of collapsed cabins, dilapidated sheds, and various gouges in the earth. Two signs with historical data complete the list.

A few miles up the Creek from Castleton is the site of Lookout. While on this stretch of road, I bumped into an interesting Hills character that called himself Two-Dollar Johnnie. He shared a wealth of knowledge regarding geology, mining and local history. He was looking for what he called "fifty-dollar rock." He was digging at a site that has been worked on and off for about 130 years. For the price of a can of soda, I received a two-hour lecture and guided tour on the gold-mining history of the Black Hills.

At one time, this was Crook City's one-room schoolhouse. More recently, it has served as a private residence.

CROOK CITY (Lawrence)

This was the first town in Lawrence County and one of the oldest communities of the Black Hills. General George A. Crook camped in the valley of Whitewood Creek during the early winter of 1875. Prospectors looking for gold followed on the heels of army boots. A prospectors' camp for placer mining was born near Crook's bivouac site. Its first name was, appropriately, Crooks Camp. Soon the name changed to Crook City. It then moved two miles northeast to its present location, all in a short period. By early 1876, the first location was already a ghost, and the second, a boomer. A photo taken at the time shows a large main street with many outlying buildings totaling about one hundred, all of lumber. Sources claim a peak population of anywhere between five hundred and three thousand. The lower number appears more likely. At one point, the town had a newspaper, post office, church, school, a few civic buildings, and even a flourmill.

The town did not have much staying power. Placer deposits soon played out, and no major diggings were located in the immediate area. The *Crook City Tribune* ran its only issue on June 10, 1876. The schoolhouse that had been built to replace a rented log cabin burned down in the 1880s. This was replaced by a one-room schoolhouse built of stone. It still stands today and is used as a private residence.

This private road leads to the site of Crook City's sawmill.

Living in Crook City was rough. When the town boomed, it was a rough town. When it went bust, it got even rougher for those who stayed. In the best of times, it was isolated, and winters were harsh. Indian attacks were a constant danger. By 1878, the town had already passed its peak. By 1900, only a post office and twenty-seven residents were left.

At first, the railroad bypassed Crook City. This hastened the town's decline. In 1886, when the Fremont, Elkhorn and Missouri Valley Railroad finally laid tracks to Crook City, it was just a small farming town. By then, L.W. Valentine and J. L. Denman claimed most of the old town site as a homestead. The old railroad bed is still visible from Whitewood.

Late in Crook City's history, a sawmill was built in town to take advantage of the local timber. The mill still stands along with large piles of sawdust, bearing mute testimony to busier days. A private road named Sawmill Lane leads up from the county highway to the old mill.

By the mill and scattered along the hillside are a small number of old cabins and sheds. Some of these are of dovetailed log construction. All remains are on posted private property, but you can easily view them from the road. A good set of binoculars would be helpful.

There was a cemetery on a hill above the town, but I failed to locate it. Sources claim that this is the oldest cemetery in the Black Hills, but I have not confirmed this. The last reports claimed a number of stone markers with old historical dates. Unfortunately, the reports also come with old publishing dates. Many of the grave markers have been moved away to the Whitewood Cemetery. The Crook City Cemetery is also on private property, if it still exists.

Another claim to fame for Crook City is that it was the home of "Aunt Sally." She claimed to be the first African American woman to live in the Black Hills.

Much information obtained from books about this location was dated. Many websites were just plain wrong. The town has a small population scattered about in a few cottages.

The best way to get there is to take I-90 to Whitewood and ask for directions politely. The road to Crook City is paved and is parallel to an old railroad bed. Travel should be done from early spring through fall.

ENGLEWOOD (Lawrence)
SITE NOT VISITED

This town started as Ten Mile Ranch, a stage stop on the line to Deadwood. A still here provided both Deadwood and the stage stop with a good portion of their whiskey.

In 1891, the town became a small railroad junction and its name changed to Akin—railroad telegraphers found it easier and quicker to use one-word names. On December 2, 1892, the name changed once again, this time to Englewood.

This photo was taken from the author's campsite in Custer State Park. At the time, one of the mountain sheep fell into his camp.

A standard-gauge line passed through the town on the way to Deadwood and Spearfish. This line belonged to the Chicago, Burlington and Quincy Railroad. The railroad built a roundhouse in Englewood to service their engines. The Black Hills and Fort Pierre Railroad, one of several narrow-gauge lines that served the town of Terry, ran through here on its way to Piedmont. Both lines used this town as a fuel, water, and sand stop. The sand was used to increase traction on the steel rail lines. From Englewood, the narrow-gauge line went uphill to Terry and Trojan. The standard-gauge line went downhill to Deadwood and Lead. Locomotives for this last stretch were changed due to the steepness of the grade.

Another smaller industry in town was a generating plant. It regained some of the electrical power used to pump water from Hanna over the divide to the Homestake Mine.

Railroads started using diesel engines, negating the need to stop at Englewood for water and coal. Many mines closed, shutting down the narrow-gauge line. Now that the Homestake mine was closed, so did all of the major industries for this community. The population had been on the decline for some time. The post office closed due to lack of customers on March 31, 1943. After this, people here had to pickup their mail at Lead.

Today, a small number of maps, including the Black Hills National Forest map, still show Englewood. The National Forest map shows a small number of buildings on the west bank of Whitewood Creek. Others also show that a few structures and a small population still exist there. The easiest way to reach it is to head south on the road to Rochford—National Forest Road 17—and after a mile, turn right at Whitewood Creek onto National Forest Road 227. Drive northeast for a little more than one mile and you should be there.

FOUR MILE (Custer)

This is one of two Old West tourist ghost towns in the Black Hills that actually rest on the site of a ghost town; the other is Rockerville. They both use their old names, but the similarity ends there. Four Mile has more of a frontier style and is open for business; Rockerville is for sale.

It is claimed that the Four Mile site was first used as a temporary stockade or camp for Colonel George Armstrong Custer. The current owners of the town have what may have been the original two-seater outhouse from the post still on location. In their gift shop/museum, they proudly display evidence provided by grandchildren of a pioneer woman who lived in the stockade. Further, the location is shown on Custer's mapping of his southern exploration route.

This sign is posted at Four Mile's parking lot.

In 1876, the location became a stagecoach stop and was named "Four Mile" by the stagecoach line. This was simply because it was four miles from Custer, the beginning of the line. Other stops had equally imaginative names, such as "Nine Mile" and "Twelve Mile." The town's population of eight did not exceed its name by much.

By 1890, Four Mile had become an actual town. The name had been changed to Moss City. There was a saloon, jail, store, and a population estimated at one hundred (probably its peak). There may have been an official post office under the name of Moss City, but this is unconfirmed. Previously, the area's mail was delivered to the Four Mile stagecoach station.

Gold dredging was conducted in the adjacent Four Mile Creek in 1898 and 1933. Small piles of gravel collected from the attempt are still visible. Gold dredging met with little success. Over time the history, location, fate, and even the town's name faded away. In their examination of old postal records, others helped accidentally rediscover Moss City.

Later, in the early twentieth century, the town went back to its the original name, Four Mile, as a tiny crossroads community. It contained a small lumber operation, store, school, and a few homes sprinkled around a minor road intersection. A number of these buildings are still there.

Today, the name Four Mile refers to the tourist frontier town operation, started in 1994 by a family who had a love of local history and a dedication to preserve it. There is an open-air museum with more than fifty original or reproduced historical structures, including the reconstructed stockade. Actual wagon wheel ruts from the stagecoach days run through the site. Wooden sidewalks and numerous false-front buildings take you back to a different time.

The museum is open from mid-May until after the buffalo roundup in Custer State Park. From Memorial Day through Labor Day, the site operates escorted hayride tours. Walking tours are also conducted.

This is the entrance, gift shop, and museum of the Four Mile site.

You can do a self-guided tour with a handheld recorder, available at the gift store. There is a Wild West melodrama featured on Thursday and Friday nights. Four Mile is open whenever the owner chooses, or by appointment in the off-season. Admission is charged. Children six and under are free when accompanied by their parents.

The town is located, of course, four miles west of Custer, South Dakota, on U.S. Highway 16. This nineteenth-century re-creation has a twenty-first-century website: *http://www.fourmilesd.com*.

GALENA (Lawrence)

The town of Galena was founded during, and due to, the 1876 gold rush, even though no gold was discovered there. In 1875, while miners were prospecting for gold, a vein of galena (lead sulphide) was discovered. As is often the case, silver was found in this lead ore. There is a sign in the center of town proclaiming "Historic Mining Camp 1875." One of the first and most productive mines was the Cora. Many more mines, such as the Branch Mint, Gilt

Edge Maid, Golden Crest, Oro Hondo, and at least three named Emma, followed. The latter mine name was inspired by a young woman who worked at a local boardinghouse. Soon there were three smelters, an assay shop, a few businesses, and seventy-five residents.

Galena was a town with a number of ups and downs. The first boom lasted from 1876 to 1887. Major litigation caused the first downer. A significant person in Galena's early history and economy was a man named Colonel J. H. Davey. He came to the Hills in 1878 with little money and a lot of ambition. After a short time, he acquired the lease to the Florence Mine and mill and perhaps also the Sitting Bull. He successfully worked the properties and expanded the operation. In 1883, he enlarged the mill to twenty stamps and added a sizable smelter. One year later, Davey entered into litigation with the Richmond Company, which caused all of his properties to cease operations. It was the first blow to the economy of Galena. After a number of years and a trip to the U.S. Supreme Court, Davey gave up in frustration. He abandoned his Black Hills mining properties and headed for the gold fields of Idaho.

Many interesting structures still stand in backyards or are half-hidden in the forest.

The next blow to Galena came when the bottom fell out of the silver market. When the price of silver fell, so did the fortunes of many western mining towns. In 1895, the price of silver rose, and so briefly did Galena. The mines involved in the Davey-Richmond litigation stayed closed. This second boom was short-lived, lasting only until 1897.

This second bust killed a planned major expansion here. In 1897, the Union Hill Mining Company purchased numerous properties in the area, including a large building to install a two hundred–stamp mill. The stamps were never installed. The price of silver fell that year, killing the whole project. After spending a good deal of money and doing little or no mining, the company pulled out. After the turn of the century most mining in Galena centered on lead instead of silver.

In 1892, a school was built here; the building remains today as a registered historical landmark. It has undergone a recent and thorough renovation.

The railroads provided a third economic stimulus. In 1902, the Deadwood Central Railroad ran a narrow-gauge branch line through town. Another narrow-gauge route crossed through Galena. Jim Hardin, owner of the Branch Mint Mine, operated this line. The line ran from the Branch Mint Mill to a number of area mines, including the Gilt Edge Maid. The Deadwood Central railroad line at Galena was abandoned in 1912.

By this time, the place had been generally deforested. With all the building construction, bridges, railroad ties, mine beams, and the use of wood for fuel, the need for timber stripped the Black Hills of its tree cover. A good number of other towns sprouted up in the area. They used the smelters at Galena and other services. Their names tell us little: Bion, Bear Butte, Gibraltar, Griggs, North Galena, Richmond, Strawberry Gulch, and Virginia City; their names are all that are left.

Today, there is a small year-round population here occupying about a dozen cabins along with the usual summer cottages. One website claims a zero population, but that is plain wrong. There are no services offered in Galena. The location can be found on Black Hills National Forest map, along with a small number of other maps and atlases. The whole area is still full of mining claims, some of which are currently active. In the 1970s, the Golden Crest mine had the water pumped out to restart mining operations. Mining has never completely left the district.

There are a fair number of original structures around the site. They range from lying collapsed on the ground to being completely rebuilt for modern use. Some are being used as barns, sheds, or outhouses. I was pointed to one cabin that is supposed to be from 1877 and the oldest structure standing. Locals claimed the cabin belonged to one of the original prospectors. He did not find enough silver and moved on to Colorado, where he struck it rich with a benzinite mine and in the hotel business. There is the old livery's barn, the blacksmith shop, and the 1892 school. There are some mine tailings at one end of town. A few stone foundations lie around town, begging more questions than they answer. The glory hole of the Gilt Edge Maid Mine might still be visible.

To find Galena, head south from Pluma on U.S. Highway 385 for about five miles. At the top of Strawberry Hill, turn east on a gravel road and follow the signs, going northeast for another two miles. The last couple of miles to Galena are on a fair gravel road. Still it is best to travel the area roads when they are dry. The best time to visit is from spring through fall.

Opposite page, top: The residents of Galena are proud of their history. On my last visit, one citizen even volunteered to take me on a tour of the town.

Opposite page, bottom: This barn may have been the town's livery stable at one time.

This page, top: A resident in town pointed this structure out to me and claimed it was the first cabin built in Galena.

This page, bottom: This was the Galena School. It has been restored and is on the National Register of Historic Places.

LOOKOUT (Pennington)

The town of Lookout was born in 1882 with the discovery of Lookout Mine. J. T. Hooper and F. J. Ayers located the mine. There was probably already a small mining camp at this part of the valley, but no name was recorded. Some claim the original name was Fort Lookout, but this appears unlikely for a number of reasons, the least of which is there was never a fort here. The Lookout mine is located high above the old town site on the side of a small mountain. As with many other mines in the Castle Creek Basin, the miners here were looking for gold.

The town grew quickly. In 1884, the Fish and Hunter Saw Mill opened. The Robinson & Hawgood's Spread Eagle mine opened and, in addition, used 126 men to dig a ditch. The purpose of the ditch was to catch and divert water for power to both the Lookout mill and the Spread Eagle mine.

The town was full of cabins, saloons, shops, and stores. The population peaked at an estimated six hundred between 1884 and

This is an old section of a hand-dug water flume that helped provide hydropower for Lookout Mill.

1886. Sometime between 1882 and 1890, the forty-stamp mill from the Alta Lodi Company of Myersville was moved here. The mill was either expanded or added to an existing one because this location is a fifty-stamper. A tramway was built up the mountain to the Lookout mine. Ore came from the Lookout mine tramway, the Spread Eagle, and numerous claims in the Castle Creek Valley. In 1890, the governor of New Hampshire and a few of his friends bought the Lookout mill, mine, and tramway. By this time, the town had only the mill, a post office, few if any businesses, and fifty-seven stubborn residents. Most of the district's mines had closed.

These are collapsed remains of Lookout Mill.

Since the mill ran on waterpower, it had to close during times of drought or freezing. In winter, the town would close; basically the entire population sat it out in Deadwood until spring. This movement was not an uncommon seasonal event for several western mining towns. It is claimed that at Lookout, residents left most of their possessions behind with no fear of theft. Whether this is due to local character or harsh winters is open to conjecture.

The biggest problem was not water or winter but the lack of high-grade ore. The mill stopped operations in 1905 when the last gold was hauled out of the Lookout mine. The other mining operations had already shut down. There is still gold in that valley today, but usually it is not even worth fifty dollars a ton for the ore.

All that remains today are the dilapidated ruins of a large mill, remnants of a tramway that leads up a mountain to the old Lookout Mine, a vertical mineshaft with a collapsed mine head (dangerous), a number of pits with buildings, dugouts, or where prospecting was done, and fragments of a water flume that runs along the north side of Castle Creek.

To find Lookout, head south from Mystic for one mile on County Road 231. Turn west on Castle Creek Road at Castleton. Drive four miles up a scenic canyon. This road is not on most maps of the Black Hills, but the turnoff is well marked.

Since 1887, this has been an on-and-off gold mining operation at Lookout Mill.

This is an open and dangerous vertical mineshaft at Lookout Mill.

The Natural Forest Campground at Castle Peak is in the vicinity. There are several old mining sites in this area. These mine locations are above the old town site of Lookout and probably used the Lookout Mill. This is a very good area for hiking and photography.

MAITLAND (Lawrence)

There is not much left to this town, especially considering its peak size and its duration as a mining town. Maitland began as Garden City sometime before 1900. There was a large and unsuccessful chlorination mill run by the Garden City Company, hence the town's first name. This was a small mining town that served the area's many gold mines. The Beltram, Columbus, Eagle, Echo, and Penobscot were among the many active mines of the time. Alexander Maitland, ex-governor of Michigan, bought the Penobscot mine in April 1902 and proceeded to develop the operation. Both the Penobscot mine and Garden City took his last name.

By January 1, 1903, a forty-ton stamp mill was in operation. It is possible and likely the mill also processed ore from the area's other mines. The ore at the Maitland mine had to be roasted and then put through a cyanide separation process before thirty dollars worth of gold could be extracted from a ton of rock. Mines in this district were shaft mines of hard rock. As always, it was hot, dirty, and dangerous

These are the foundations of a mill or smelter at Maitland.

This early twentieth-century excavator has been parked here so long that trees are now growing through it.

work. The Maitland mine was the area's principle mine and operated under various managers until 1915. It reopened briefly under the Canyon Corporation during 1935–36.

In the 1950s, the main mill accidentally burned down while being dismantled in a salvage operation. At its peak, Maitland had more than fifty homes and businesses, more than a dozen mine buildings, and a couple hundred residents. The site is approximately 2 1/2 miles northwest of Central City along False Bottom Creek. The best way to Maitland is to take U.S. Highway 85 to National Forest Road 195 just outside of Central City. This is a good all-weather gravel road that runs up Blacktail Gulch.

The mining history may be long, but old-time remains are in short supply. The stamp mill's stone foundation is the main find. It is made of undressed native rock and cement. One cabin of questionable vintage is now paired with a mobile home and one other shed or cabin. An old earth-moving machine shovel and a small amount of mining debris round out the list. The cabin has a concrete foundation and electric wiring, while the piece of machinery had rubber tires. That means that these remains are from the Canyon Corporation operation. During my visit, the main mine site was being bulldozed as part of a cleanup or a new surface mine. Either way, the bulldozer has cleared more than just dirt.

MOON (Pennington)

Moon is located on the western edge of the Black Hills National Forest at the intersection of County Roads 117 and 301. There is a small, primitive National Forest compound by the same name conveniently next door. The town and campground are in a very beautiful and remote setting. And at 6,400 feet, they are some of the higher ones in the Black Hills.

The town was incorporated around the turn of the century, and it served the area's farmers. Moon was never a large or important settlement. With the increased preeminence of the automobile and

It can be a pleasant drive to Moon, although at 6,400 feet, snow may cover the road through June.

The site of Moon has the advantage of having a campground adjacent to it.

The remains of Moon are now a summer cottage community. The building at the far right has served as the town store, gas station, and post office.

roads being built elsewhere, Moon faded away slowly, and by the middle of the century it was deserted.

Today, the site consists of about a half-dozen perfectly preserved original buildings underneath the forest canopy. The buildings appear to be summer cottages now. One of these once held a store, gas station and post office together. Now, it is reported to be a hunter's cabin. The place is usually snowbound in winter, making the roads inaccessible except by snowmobile.

This is the last of several small mills in the gold-mining community of Myersville.

MYERSVILLE (Pennington)

Myersville was founded as a hard-rock gold-mining town before, or in, 1883. It was named after John Myers, an early area miner and lumberman, and was originally called Myers City. The population quickly peaked at about 150. At this time, the main employer was the Alta Lodi Mining Company. It had built a forty-stamp mill in the area, but it did not locate enough ore to keep it busy. Myersville's sister community was Alta; it lay on the east side of Myersville and was often considered the same place. The Alta mine was located here, surrounded by the very small town and probably the mill. Eventually, the mill was dismantled and moved to Lookout where the remains are still today. Most of both towns moved with it.

From 1892 to 1917, James Cochran reworked five previous claims. He labored during the summers using a sixteen-ton Huntington mill. Another spurt of mining activity occurred between 1931 and 1936. A few small mines and scattered equipment from this period can still be seen in the woods.

Myersville is supposed to have a cemetery, which it probably shared with Alta, but I failed to locate it. The town is about 2 1/2 miles southwest of Rochford on the Castle Peak Road. This road also leads to the Forest Service fire lookout on Castle Peak, but the tower is no longer used. The road is easy to miss and I did, twice; it is a small spur on the west side of County Road 305 and, at first glance, appears to be a farm road. About one mile south of here is another road, National Forest Road 181, with a sign reading "Castle Peak C.G." and an arrow pointing left. This is a campground and not the correct road to Myersville.

Once on the correct road, the setting becomes pastoral. Some of the farm buildings are from a much earlier time and are being used for something other than originally intended. A few modern homes and summer cottages are interspersed. There is a small mill and a large two-story house. The machinery from the mill is gone; the empty shell that remains is too small to be the old Alta Lodi mill site. This might have been the Huntington mill used by James Cochran, although it is more likely this was the small cyanide mill located in Myersville. The well-built two-story house speaks of something more than a common miner's dwelling. Most likely, it was the home of a manager, supervisor, or owner of a mill or mine. A safe with a missing door lies in the front yard. Land scars above the town show signs of mining.

This was the largest house during the town's boom period.

This safe, with its door torn off, slowly rusts away in the underbrush.

Both the mill and the first floor of the two-story house have been stripped down to the bare frame for their boards. Stripping old buildings for their material has been a common practice since man built his first hut. Photos from 1974 show that the house was vacant, but in good condition with the window shutters still intact.

County Road 305 from Rochford is a good gravel road. The Castle Peak road is dirt through Myersville and turns into a rough rock surface as it ascends Castle Peak.

MYSTIC (Pennington)

Mystic began in 1876 as a placer gold-mining camp along Castle Creek. The town was originally called Sitting Bull, but the name was changed in 1889 when the Chicago, Burlington and Quincy Railroad came through. Mystic was also the western terminal for the narrow-gauge Rapid City, Black Hills and Western Railway. The railroads were initially a boom and opened up the Black Hills completely. The railroad tracks for the Rapid City, Black Hills and Western Railway in Mystic were ripped up and sold for scrap in 1947. Frequent floods and fires had made the operation unprofitable. The last Burlington Northern freight train ran through town in November 1983. Today, old railroad beds, bridges, and the like are still visible all over the Hills area.

In 1904, the Electro-Chemical Reduction Company set up a large and advanced gold reclamation plant. The plant was an experimental operation that extracted gold by a chlorination process. It cost about a million dollars to assemble the operation. The plant was a

The site of Mystic is surrounded by numerous mines. Some of these mines are operating today; many are old, and all should be considered dangerous to enter.

failure. It was torn down and its foundations used for the Frink Saw Mill. The sawmill operated from 1919 to 1952. When the sawmill closed, the town lost its last major employer. The mill is now gone, and the foundation rests alone next to a parking lot.

Mining never completely left the area. Some mining occurred right in town, and the remains from it are still there. Many mining claims have been worked and reworked numerous times. Walking over the site, you notice nails, tools, wood, and construction techniques from all different time periods. In one mining trench, I found the frame of a 1920s pickup truck.

Just out of sight from County Road 231 are a small number of mineshafts built during the 1876 rush. Mine ruins and debris heavily litter the area. These include the collapsed remains of Brown's cabin that lie next to the Fortune Seekers mine. The cabin was the first building in Mystic and is a nationally registered landmark. Most sources mention an abandoned sawmill, school, and store—the Frink Saw Mill, the Hays Brothers store, which later became the school, and the William Frick Grocery. Only the foundations of these three buildings remain.

Today, the community of Mystic consists of a church, summer cottages, a trailhead, and assorted shacks. The church, the Mecahan Memorial Chapel, is a beautiful and well-preserved log structure. It was built as a Presbyterian house of worship with the materials and labor provided by the Frink Saw Mill and the town of Mystic. Interestingly, the sawmill provided unhewn

Top: This is the Mecahan Memorial Chapel, a registered national historic site.

Bottom: These are original boom-period structures. Their histories are posted at the trail shelter.

These trenches, whether dug as mine pits or water flumes, are an archeologist's or historian's dream. They were choked with debris.

logs for the building. Oscar Donaldson, a Presbyterian missionary, was the church's first pastor. The chapel is now a registered national historic site.

An old garage and icehouse are across the street from the church. Three more buildings lie on the ground dismantled; these are original structures, and there are plans to reassemble them in the near future. There is an intersection next to this group of buildings. Turning off the main road, take the secondary road to a trailhead and the rest of the town's remains. The road ends after flanking Castle Creek and the Mickelson Trail for a few miles. The trail uses the old Burlington Northern railbed. The trailhead has a parking lot, pit toilet, and a pavilion with historical displays, including a map of the town's original layout and much of its history. Four old original buildings stand nearby with a sign stating what each one was. The sign shows a fifth building labeled as a blacksmith shop. That building was not standing on my last visit; it may now be one of the many piles of used lumber lying around. A foundation of one of Mystic's first stores is included in the grouping. A quarter mile along the road past the pavilion are the bare remains of a railroad section house and a number of additional foundations.

Most of the houses in this town appear to be of the rehabbed summer cottage variety. There may not be a year-round population. Mystic is situated on County Road 231 about twelve miles north of Hill City. The location is marked on all area maps.

PRESTON (Lawrence)
SITE NOT VISITED

Preston was one of the towns that sprang up around Ragged Top Mountain in 1897. Gold ore was found at a shallow depth in this area. The other towns in this group were Balmoral, Cyanide, Dacy, and Victoria.

Local tradition claims that the gold deposits were discovered by one Mr. Preston, who noticed a chunk of ore stuck in his horse's shoe. Some of the diggings contained high-grade ore and made several good mines, including the Ulster and the Spearfish Gold Mining and Milling Company. The ore was not extensive, though, and the mines soon played out. The Spearfish Mine operated from 1899 to 1906 and produced 48,618 ounces of gold. The Ulster, which was one mile north of town, operated around the same time. The majority of the larger mines operated from 1896 to 1915.

A simple ore chute in Mystic.

The town had a newspaper, the *Ragged Top Shaft*, for a short time. Preston and its neighbors no longer appear on the National Forest map, but Ragged Top Mountain does. The roads around the mountain are mostly dirt and make for poor driving when wet. As far as directions, you must be able to find Ragged Top Mountain on a map and use a topographic map to find your way there. The roads from Trojan are closed due to recent mining. Therefore, you must approach Preston over a great distance of bad roads from the north or via Spearfish Canyon.

Preston and Balmoral were supposed to be a quarter mile apart. This would not have been uncommon for towns to bump into each other and still have separate identities, just as they do today. Time has obscured facts, names, and boundary lines. There is some controversy as to which location is which. Some claim Preston is located to the left and Balmoral to the right; others state the opposite. Some say they are the same site and so is Cyanide, to boot.

The Ragged Top School is supposed to be here or at Balmoral, or in between. There are probably no remains of the neighboring town of Dacy. The mining district was served by a maze of narrow-gauge lines, and the old railroad beds would still be there.

The entire site may have disappeared due to a large open-pit mining operation being conducted by Wharf Mining Company.

PRINGLE (Custer)

This semi-ghost town began as a mining town. It then became a center for the timber industry. Both industries rollercoastered the town through time, and both still exist here in small ways. One of the most recent mine booms was for Feldspar; you can still see the mine in a hill overlooking the town. The railroad came and passed through the town in time too.

Today, Pringle is a small town with less than one hundred residents. It caters mostly to tourists and elk hunters. It has a small saloon, post office, and church. False fronts and log cabin structures are

fairly common. On my last visit, the town's only store, "The Trading Post," had just gone out of business. There were many more businesses when this town was a railroad stop. More buildings are vacant than are occupied. Structures, whether occupied or vacant, are from both the nineteenth and twentieth centuries. It is easy to see that a number of structures have been occupied and reoccupied several times. A log cabin with modern windows is in a current state of collapse. This is to be expected because of the cycle of boom-and-bust economies.

The railroad tracks were taken for scrap metal in the 1980s. You can still see where the train went through town. The old railbed, abandoned grain elevator, and a hiking shelter all show the way the train used to come and go. Now it is hikers; the old railbed has been converted into a hiking trail. Old sidewalks reveal where whole blocks have faded away. A ramshackled timber mill sits astride the highway, giving the appearance of infrequent use at best. Abandoned mines of various ages surround the town.

Pringle sits quietly on the intersection of U.S. Highway 385 and State Highway 89.

Top: There is a lot of vacant housing in Pringle, and it covers many time periods.

Middle: The silo still stands, but the railroad tracks are gone.

Bottom: With the tracks ripped up, the old railbed has been converted into the George S. Mickelson Trail.

Opposite page, top: The large front windows indicate this was probably a business building in Pringle.

Opposite page, bottom: Timber has been one of Pringle's boom-and-bust industries.

REDFERN (Pennington)

Don't blink, or you'll miss this one. Redfern is a minor site two miles north of Tigerville. It was a small section town on the Burlington railroad. It was established in 1891 or 1892 and named after Albert Redfern, a railroad man who helped build the section house. The section was the Hill City–Deadwood line and followed the old Mickelson Trail. The old railroad bed is still visible today.

The town had a brief boom in the 1950s, when it was the home of the now defunct Black Hills Silica Sand Corporation. The remains here consist of a few cabins of questionable history, an abandoned boxcar that was used as a house, a broken sign, debris, and the railroad bed. It is on private property but is easily viewable from National Forest Road 231 (County Road 318). This is a good gravel road. The location is marked on the Black Hills National Forest map.

ROCHFORD (Pennington)

Rochford got started as a gold-mining town in February 1877. It was named after one of its three founders, M. D. Rochford. A hunting party had accidentally discovered gold ledges on Montezuma Hill in August 1876. The party included Rochford, Richard B. Hughes, and William VanFleet. Rochford and Hughes returned to mine gold and start a town. In March 1877, a mining district was officially established. By December 1878, Rochford had grown to have about five hundred residents, a fairly sizable business district, a school, the rarity of canopied sidewalks, and three hundred cabins and

Top: This converted railcar is the last intact structure of the railroad section town of Redfern.

Bottom: The sign advertises the only two businesses in town.

buildings. In 1879, a twenty-stamp mill had been built in town for both the Evangeline and Minnesota mines. Soon came the Stand-By mine with a forty-stamp mill and a water flume to provide power.

A second boom came in 1889 when the Chicago, Burlington and Quincy Railroad laid tracks through Rochford while building its Custer-Deadwood route. Another mining boom swept through the area in 1896, but Rochford did not seem to notice. As always, the gold ran out. When the timber was over-harvested, the railroads lost most of their remaining business. By 1900, the town was down to just forty-eight inhabitants and a post office. The railroad tracks were torn up in 1985–86, but the track beds are still visible. One runs west in the direction of Fox Park.

Annie D. Tallent, reportedly the first white woman to settle in the Black Hills, was a prominent citizen in Rochford. She taught school and was the town's postmaster for a while. The two-story house in which she had lived at Rochford had been somewhat updated, but sadly it burned down in the late 1970s.

Rochford is situated in an idyllic forest setting in the heart of the Black Hills. A sign hanging from a rather rustic and weather-beaten building states that the population is twenty-five. The structure was probably once a saloon. These days, a sign says the building is the Rochford Mall. Looming over the town is the overgrown foundation of the Stand-By mill. The mill

Top: This picture of the Rochford Mall was taken in 1997. The building was for sale.

Bottom: This photo of the Rochford Mall was taken in 2005. The building has been extensively rehabbed since my first visit.

itself, which is highlighted in so many books and on so many websites, is not there and has not been for a couple of decades. It was a huge, imposing structure that dominated the town. With time, the building had become dangerous and was torn down in the 1980s. The location also has a beautifully reworked church, a new elementary school, old homes, cabins, and shacks. Most of the buildings here, occupied or vacant, are from the early boom period. Most of the town's houses are reworked miners' cabins or old saloons. Structures built of logs are common. Above you, numerous mineshafts peer out from Montezuma Hill bearing mute testimony to busier days. Do not be tempted. These mines are on private property and dangerous. Stay away from them.

Remaining among the more famous buildings are the Irish Gulch Dance Hall and the historic Moonshine Gulch Saloon. The Irish Gulch has recently been rebuilt with a steel roof and stucco walls and no longer has its western appearance. I had seen it before the rebuild; it looked straight out of a television western. Moonshine Gulch Saloon is still open for business and serves a good cheeseburger. This is the place to ask for local directions to other ghost towns, campgrounds, and the like. The Rochford Chapel is fully restored and still used, although on an irregular basis.

Rochford may be reached from Deadwood via U.S. Highway 85 to County Road 17. Head south for fourteen miles. An old railbed will lead you into town. This used to be the Burlington line and followed the route of the Mickelson Trail. Today, it is a hiking path. From Hill City head north sixteen miles: first on County Road 17 and then right onto Forest Service Road 231. This route takes you through Castleton and Mystic. Both routes are scenic.

ROCKERVILLE (Pennington)

This is a ghost town within a ghost town. Rockerville is a small highway stop that has mostly gone out of business. The biggest business in town is, or was, an old western days tourist town—a mixture of old and new, such as a blacksmith shop and sheriff's

Opposite page, top : There are a fair number of vacant homes in Rochford.

Opposite page, bottom: This building dates from Rochford's boom days. It has been thoroughly rebuilt. It was a business, but it was not the Irish Gulch Dance Hall as the sign claims. Today, it is a residence.

This page, top: The sign claims this is the University of Rochford.

Middle: Some boom-period housing in Rochford has been rehabbed into summer cottages.

Bottom: Even some of Rochford's newer housing, such as this one with a satellite dish, is vacant.

Right: This was once a booming tourist attraction.

Top: The majority of the town of Rockerville was for sale on my last visit.

Bottom: Some of these structures are original and were moved here. Most were newly constructed on the site.

office, flanked by places selling snow cones and cotton candy. Some of the buildings there today were moved from other ghost towns in the early 1950s, but most of the buildings are re-creations of the past. The site chosen had been the location for a mining ghost town in the past, but all original remains had vanished; only the name was kept. The main reason for picking this location was the location. It is situated on U.S. Highway 16 between Rapid City and Mount Rushmore and can be located on the state map.

Today, the old is mixed with the new. The Old West town is still there and so is some scattered new construction. The tourist town operates on an intermittent basis. The latest population statistics I could locate stated only two people lived there. In 1992, both old and new Rockerville were posted for sale. On my last visit in 2004, both the Old West town and business sections were for sale again, or still. The business section for sale consisted of a motel, café, RV park, pool, and a store with gas pumps. The Old West town had a laundry mat, an RV park, and a store.

Rockerville began like many other towns in the area—during the 1876 Black Hills gold rush. Gold was discovered here in December 1876 when one William Keeler became snowbound and started panning to fight boredom. He was on an unnamed branch of Spring

Creek and soon joined by two other panners, Bart Henderson and D. G. Silliman. At this point nothing more is to be heard of William Keeler and it was left to others to make this place boom. Captain Jack Crawford found gold in Spring Creek itself in March 1877. His discovery and the lack of water in the creek gave the place its first name: Captain Jack's Dry Diggins. The second discovery is what actually gave birth to this mining camp. Due to the lack of water here, rockers were used to conserve the precious stuff and to separate the gold from the place's sticky clay deposits. For this reason, it was given its second name, Rockville. Several attempts were made to construct flumes to bring in more water for the placer deposits. Between miners and construction workers, the town swelled to one hundred buildings and one thousand residents by 1880.

There were several companies with numerous flume projects. One of the first was the Black Hills Placer Mining Company, formed in 1878 with capital from people and companies in eastern states. This was a huge project with up to seventeen miles of ditches, trestles, and wooden flumes. It is claimed that about five million boards of lumber were used in its construction. First, a dam had to be built upstream on Spring Creek near Sheridan. The actual construction

Top: Most buildings were grouped in clusters, although some stood alone.

Bottom: These buildings served as restrooms, a bathhouse, and laundry facilities for a small RV court.

Left: A handful of abandoned homes surround the vacant tourist town attraction.

Top: This portion of Rockerville actually looks like a fairly authentic 1880s western town.

Bottom: Even this motel was for sale.

of the flume began in 1880. The cost was initially estimated at $198,500, but ended up being closer to $300,000.

That was not the only setback; the flume leaked badly. Every time the flume leaked, the company lost money. The company hired Ben Rush full-time just to locate and patch leaks. Rush walked the flume grade and used rags to plug the leaks. He also shoveled a wagon full of horse manure every day to seal the cracks. This must have made him a matter of some discussion with the local miners. The leaks came from another problem: the company had used green lumber.

The operation was managed locally by Ambrose Bierce, who later became famous as a writer. The operation produced $500,000 worth of gold—money for the company—but, due to mismanagement and numerous problems, it still ran in the red. A series of court rulings against the Black Hills Placer Mining Company finally forced it out of business. On December 30, 1882, it was sold for the paltry sum of five dollars. Though the flume was not a boon for the Black Hills Company, it and the other flumes were a tremendous boost to Rockerville's total economy.

This town had a reputation of being one of the rowdiest mining camps in the Black Hills. In March 1879, the name was changed again to Rockerville. This was done in a very American way—by petition. To make it official, the petitions were submitted to the U.S. Postal Service.

Rockerville's boom peaked in the late summer of 1880. Then, all of the flumes failed and the placer deposits played out. The miners moved out and Rockerville became a true ghost town. By the 1930s,

Rockerville was a gas station stop. A stone chimney from one of the miner's cabins was one of the only remains. Today, traces of the water flumes leading from Lake Sheridan are the only original remains.

ROUBAIX (Lawrence)

There is not much here to recommend this place to a ghost town hunter. Still, it appears in virtually all books and on all websites dealing with Black Hills ghost towns. When you arrive all you will find is a small bedroom and summer cottage community. There are virtually no remains of its glory days.

Roubaix was founded in 1876 along Elk Creek as a gold mining town and originally called Perry. At first a placer-mining camp with a one-stamp mill, it soon turned to hard-rock mining. The Uncle Sam, Roubaix's major mine, opened in 1878. It is claimed that the town was also called Uncle Sam at this time. (One source claimed the town was called Uncle Sam before it was called Perry. This could not be true because the Uncle Sam mine did not open until 1878, whereas the town was founded in 1876. You would not name a town after a mine that did not exist yet.) The Uncle Sam mine closed in 1880 and soon filled with water. Soon after, a forest fire destroyed a major portion of town.

In 1889, a Frenchman named Pierre Wibeaux bought the Uncle Sam mine and changed its name to the Clover Leaf. At this time, the CB&Q railroad arrived and asked for another name change to avoid confusion with the town of Terry just to the north. Wibeaux changed the name to Roubaix, after his hometown in France.

Ore from the mines was easily separated from the waste rock and only required a mercury amalgamation process to get 90 percent of the gold out of it. This same type of ore was also easy pickings for the miners. Their habit of picking out choice nuggets, also known as "high grading," cut heavily into the operation's profit margin.

A large ninety-stamp mill opened and the town quickly rebounded to a population of about five hundred. Its peak occurred probably around 1899. At the time, there was a post office, barbershop, town hall, school, newspaper, boardinghouses, churches, and a number of stores in town. There was a hospital, but I am not sure when it operated. A photo from 1903 shows the hospital, a small frame structure, in the heart of the business district.

In 1905, heavy rains led to mine flooding. The water rose to the seventh level of the mine and caused the cave-in of the shaft leading to the pumps. With no water flowing into the pumps, the motors burned out. The whole mine then flooded. Since it appeared there was no way to pump the water out, the operation was abandoned. A fire in 1905 destroyed a large section of the business district; it was not rebuilt.

In 1934, the Anaconda Gold Mining and Milling Company of Rapid City bought the property and managed to pump the water out. In September 1935, mining operations resumed but were short lived. Only ten thousand dollars worth of gold was recovered in this operation. The mine was sold for taxes in 1947.

Roubaix survives today as a small community with no services. Its location is two miles east of U.S. Highway 385 on Nemo Road. The large mill site is no longer visible. The only remains are old structures converted to modern use or new buildings that used "recovered" materials from old buildings.

SILVER CITY (Pennington)
SITE NOT VISITED

Silver City is a lake resort that uses the name, location, and many original buildings of an 1870s mining town. A number of structures have been rebuilt into summer cottages, and the whole site is on private property.

In 1874, this area along Rapid Creek was called Elkhorn Prairie by General Custer. The Gorman brothers—Jack, Luke, and Tom—came after him. They discovered two silver mines nearby, naming them the Diana and Lady of the Hills. The area was then known as Camp Gorman. Next, a town site was laid out and registered in the name of Silver City, due of course to the silver mines in the area. It quickly became a silver mining town and remained active for a number of years.

The site is also home to several legends of lost mines. One legend originates with the Gorman brothers. It says an eastern syndicate offered the brothers $300,000 for their claims. The men wanted a half million, but being uneducated, they could not figure out which amount was greater. While the brothers tried to understand the math of the offer, tragedy struck. Their cabin caught fire and the oldest brother burned to death. Strangely, the two surviving brothers disappeared and were never heard from again. The location of their mines disappeared with them.

Another legend features a lost gold mine located in an area near the town called "the Unknown Land." The mine belonged to a man named Scruton—or was it three brothers again! Supposedly, Scruton—or the Scruton brothers—showed up in Silver City producing gold nuggets and a big story to go along with them. He, or they, died before revealing the source of the gold nuggets.

The Silver City resort is located at the head of Pactola Lake and divided by Rapid Creek. It is about three miles west of U.S. Highway 385 if you take National Forest Road 299. This is a paved road that intersects with National Forest Road 251 in town. The Black Hills National Forest map shows a road heading northwest out of town for about one mile to an abandoned mine. Silver City is on all area maps and atlases, even the state highway map. One source claims you can reach the resort by taking a boat over the lake, but I cannot confirm this. Maps show the town up Rapid Creek a good distance. Also, recently drought has radically lowered the lake, making such a boat ride impossible, at least at this time. The lake route traces the old Black Hills and Western Railroad right-of-way. On this

Above: This was the caretaker's house at Spokane.

Bottom: This is the road to Spokane. It is currently gated, so a short hike is required.

same route and now under Pactola Lake itself is the previous site of another silver mining town from the same period. The town's name was Pactola, and it died a watery death when the lake was born.

SPOKANE (Custer)

Spokane started in 1890 as a mine and an accompanying small town. An alphabet soup of minerals was mined here. The long list includes lead, silver, gold, and zinc. In the milling process, small amounts of arsenic, beryl, copper, graphite, hematite, and mica were recovered as side products. The mine operated on and off for decades and was modernized at least once. A caretaker looked after the mine during in its inactive period. He was provided with a house and lived on the site year-round.

In addition to the mine, there was a mill, machine shops, a mine office, and a school. The teacher was provided with a small one-room cabin on the edge of town. The mill probably also processed ore from nearby mines. Some time after the mid-1970s, the mining

stopped permanently. The caretaker left and the Forest Service took control of the site.

Spokane's location is marked on the Black Hills National Forest map. The site is near the intersection of Iron Mountain Road, U.S. Highway 16A, and County Road 330. Turn onto the county road from the highway, and almost immediately, there is a gated dirt road on the right. Spokane is about a half-mile down this road. The mill, mine administrative offices, head frame, hoisting, and machine shops have been removed. All had been in operating order as late as 1975. Today, the barn, the caretaker's house, school, miners' shacks, the powder magazine, foundations, cisterns, pits, abandoned autos, and collapsed buildings litter an area of about ten acres. Private property abuts this spot on two sides. The teacher's cabin has been made into a summer cottage and sits on private property nearby.

TEDDY BEAR (Pennington)

This was probably never more than a small mining camp. Even though this is not a ghost town per se, the number of remains and the fact that Teddy Bear is such a good representation of the hundreds of Black Hills mining camps bear mentioning. Mining camps differed from mining towns in that the camps had few or no services. They usually had just the mine, mining equipment buildings, a number of miners' cabins, sheds, outhouses, and not much more. Camps may have had a blacksmith shop, barn, or one company store sometimes, but that is all. Teddy Bear appears to be a good example of this.

Teddy Bear's history is very sketchy and based mostly on personal observation. The hand-hewn logs and other construction techniques date this location to well before the 1900s. The town of Lookout, just a few miles away, had a lumber mill by 1884. I located two horizontal hard-rock mineshafts. The amount of waste rock at one mine shows production occurred for an extended period of time. In line with the period of construction and the site's location, this was probably a gold mining camp. The ore would have been sent to

Top: Miners' cabins in Spokane were built of rough lumber and tarpaper.

Middle: I believe this was the powder magazine at Spokane.

Bottom: This was the Spokane School.

the mill at Myersville or Lookout, depending on what the years of production were.

Most of the buildings were large and had an interesting feature— basements. These were virtually unheard of in early gold-rush days. They may have been used to provide shelter from the harsh winters, to keep ice and provide cold storage in the summer, or both. I located the remains of an old sled on the site. It is possible the miners spent the winter here, although nearby Lookout shut down during this mean season.

The remains of one building showed a doublewide entrance and therefore may have been a barn or livery. Another building, now collapsed, was shown in photos as a two-story structure.

Opposite page, top: This interesting structure originally had two stories and insulated cellars.

Opposite page, bottom: The large doorway of this building indicates it might have been a barn. This type of log construction, much like a child's Lincoln log set, did not require nails and shows that the site is quite old.

Above: The large amount of rock waste shows that, at one time, there was intensive mining activity here.

Right, top: A wagon road leading to one of the old mines.

Right, middle: The piled earthen berm helps insulate the cellar.

Right, bottom: Notching logs in this way allowed construction with fewer or even no nails. This also shows the site is quite old.

The scenery is great and makes for a nice picnic stop. Others have obviously thought so. On my visit, I noticed a stone fire-ring in which previous visitors had used the 120-plus–year-old buildings for firewood! It never fails to amaze me that someone would have to be told that this is a bad thing to do. The road can be a little rough and should be saved for good weather days. Castle Creek Campground is just one or two miles southeast down the road. The best time to visit is early fall.

The site is marked on several topographic maps, atlases, and other maps, but none show it with a name. I got the location's name from the Parker and Lambert book; it is probably wrong. Its name was actually attributed to a grouping of summer cottages that no longer exist. One website claims that Teddy Bear was the name of the town itself, but it gives no source or town history. Besides, the little it does mention appears to have been plagiarized from the Parker and Lambert book. Also, since the teddy bear is named for Theodore Roosevelt, the name is not older than 1900; the town's construction was circa the 1880s. It is possible this is a second name for the place. It is also possible that it was never its name at all.

TIGERVILLE (Pennington)

This site is usually written up incorrectly. Most sources claim there are one, two or even no buildings. There is not much at Tigerville, but there are certainly more than two buildings.

Tigerville was a gold-mining town that began as Tiger City. It was a short-lived boomer built mostly around the King Solomon Mine. By 1880, there were two stores, a post office, and a population of more than two hundred.

The exact year of founding and origin of the town's name are in dispute. Some claim the

the town's name comes from the nearby Bengal Tiger Mine. (The Bengal Tiger Mine received its name from the coloring of its ore. Rust-colored quartz made orange stripes on glistening mica schist giving the rock its tiger-like appearance.) Others point out that this mine was two or three miles away. If named after a mine, the place should have been called Solomon. Another source for the name may have been the Lucky Tiger Claims #1, #2, and #3. Some sources refer to these collectively as the Lucky Tiger Mine, but they were only unpatented claims undeveloped beyond prospecting pits. These do not appear on mineralogical or other maps since they were unpatented. Local tradition states that the Lucky Tiger claims were near the town, but this is not confirmed. Neither Tiger site saw much production and the mining boom here was short-lived.

Sometime after the mining boom, a sawmill was set up here. This was common at many old mining locations in the Black Hills. When the mill closed, so did most of what was left of the town. The old mill building still remains but has been rebuilt. It spent time as an auto repair garage and is now used as a barn.

Other remains include a home, one other building, and a few scattered sheds from the sawmill days. An unused sheepers' trailer rests on blocks on the east side of town (the word "town" is being used rather loosely). Behind the trailer, out of sight in the treeline and on private property, are at least five log cabins from the town's mining days. The cabins are constructed from unhewn logs, but some have newer windows and roofs—a sure sign that these structures were occupied more than once. A small number of similarly dated sheds and outhouses complete the setting.

Opposite page: This sheepherder's wagon rests alongside the road at Tigerville.

This page: These are two of about ten boom-period structures I found. They lie deep in the woods behind fenced and posted private property.

Tigerville is about 4 1/2 miles northwest of Hill City on County Road 308. This road is paved and well marked. The first major intersection of this route is in downtown Tigerville. The intersecting road is County Road 318 and leads to Redfern, Castleton, Mystic, and Rochford.

TROJAN (Pennington)

Gold was discovered on Bald Mountain in early 1877. This, along with another strike on nearby Green Mountain, led to a rash of mines and mining towns springing up. One of these mining towns was called Portland. The name came from the nearby Portland

Mine. Fortunes were made and lost quickly. Most mining ventures in the area were one- or two-men operations. Churches, government, and town boundary lines were rare. The whole place teemed with frenzied activity resembling a disturbed ant mound.

With the passing of time, things changed. It was getting much harder to dig in the area, so mine operations began to consolidate and grow in size. By 1900, this process was well under way in the Black Hills. By 1911, the Trojan Mining Company had bought the majority of the other mining operations on Bald Mountain. The company constructed a huge mine, mill, and cyanide-leaching plant at Bald Mountain. Then, of course, they changed the town's name from Portland to Trojan. The Bald Mountain Mining Company bought out the Trojan mine operation in 1928, but the town's name did not change this time.

Along the way, more changed than just the town's name. Life settled down, and half of Trojan became a company town. The site is somewhat divided by a mountain pass. The east side was closer to Terry Peak and consisted of miner's shacks and some private businesses. The west side

Top: The mining camp of Trojan.

Bottom: This huge ore pit has consumed the majority of Trojan.

of the pass contained the company town and was adjacent to the mill. On the whole, construction on the east side of the pass was older.

The entire mining district was crisscrossed with a patchwork of narrow-gauge railways. Many of these railbeds should still be visible today. The tracks were taken up in 1960. Even rails in the mines were removed. Today, most large-scale mining operations use huge truck-like earthmovers instead of narrow-gauge trains.

In 1959, the Portland mine closed down due to lack of profitability. Extraction costs had risen with the depth of the mine, and besides that, the ore here is low-grade. When the mine and mill closed, Trojan lost its reason for being. Millions of dollars worth of both gold and silver had come out of Bald Mountain for eighty-two years.

People tried to revive the local economy through the tourist industry. Nearby Terry Peak was selected for a snow-skiing location. Slopes were cleared and a ski lift was constructed, but the enterprise has met with only limited success. While the winter wind has been consistent, the snow has not.

Wharf Mining Company bought Bald Mountain and other neighboring mine properties in the late twentieth century. It is now mining the entire district on a grand scale. The company is excavating a couple of huge open-pit mines, which are served by the company's own network of roads. These roads are closed to public traffic and for a simple reason: the ore carriers that operate here are gigantic and once rolling, do not stop easily. This system is now used instead of narrow-gauge trains. It is much more cost-effective. Still, I miss the

Top: The building with the false front was a business, maybe a company store. The other buildings are miners' cabins.

Bottom: Enormous ore carriers have replaced the narrow-gauge railroads.

trains. On the other hand, I have seen places in Idaho that still use pack mules to haul supplies in and ore out.

There are four roads into Trojan; at least two were closed to the public on my visit. I turned west off of U.S. Highway 85, just south of Lead at Fantail Creek Gulch. This road leads up the mountain to Trojan. A small mountain pass divides the town's remains into two locations. On the east side, there are two shacks and some collapsed remains of others. They are mixed in with modern-day construction that is taking over the area. The west side has one street remaining, with about a dozen buildings standing. The only one not in a state of disrepair is a three-story red frame structure that has served as a hotel and as a headquarters for different companies. The huge mill and plant are gone. A gigantic open-mine pit has swallowed up most of what was once the town of Trojan. It appears the last major portion is endangered and may share the same fate.

The western portion of the site is posted private property and should be viewed from the public road. Be careful—there is a crossing gate here because a road for ore carriers crosses at this spot. The gate is automatic, and the ore carrier is huge. Neither the gate nor the carrier is very good at stopping for others, so you must stop for them.

VICTORIA (Lawrence)
SITE NOT VISITED

Victoria was yet another gold-mining town in the Ragged Top Mining District. It and the Victoria Mine both got their names from their parent, the Victoria Gold Mining and Milling Company. This may have been a company town. There was also a small mercury mine for a short time, but nothing came of it.

Victoria existed on several levels of Spearfish Canyon. A small settlement existed on the canyon floor and was called Lower

Top: This Trojan building has served as a school, company headquarters, and maybe a hotel.

Bottom: Today, this building in Trojan serves as the mine office for Wharf Resources.

Victoria. Also near the bottom, but farther up, were the mill and a few mill workers' houses. Above the mill, perched atop the divide between Squaw Creek and Spearfish Canyon, was the Victoria Mine. Like the rest of the mines in the Ragged Top District, the ores here were from shallow surface diggings. This is rugged terrain, and the mine had to be serviced by an aerial tramway. There was also a telephone line and a rough footpath running to the mine.

The settlement was serviced by the Chicago, Burlington and Quincy Railroad with a half-mile spur that branched out of the canyon. The railroad bed is still there today. It leads to the old mill site. Victoria is located about three miles north of Savoy and on the east side of the canyon. Look for old railbeds. Watch for the spur line; follow it a quarter mile and you should be there.

A look at photos from the 1970s shows cabins standing but vacant and in disrepair. Construction here was mixed. Some buildings had shingled roofs, modern windows, and insulation, all framed within lumber. Others were log cabins with tin roofs. Even the tramway used a mixture of lumber and timber. The reason for this mixed use of materials may have been to hold down costs, but that is just a guess.

Besides the old railbed, remains are reported but unconfirmed. The name Victoria still appears on the Black Hills National Forest map. However, the map is ambiguous about its location and provides no additional information. The location lies approximately in the northwest corner of the Ragged Top Mining District.

Top: These are the last structures from the old mine plant at Trojan that have not been consumed by the current mining activity.

Bottom: This is one of the remaining structures from Trojan's mining days that still stands on the east side of the pass.

WYOMING

black hills ghost towns

A smaller, yet still significant part of the Black Hills rests in the State of Wyoming. Just as in the South Dakota portion of the Hills, there are ghost towns here. I have visited all the sites in Wyoming listed in this book.

The towns usually began and faded for pretty much the same reasons as the old boomtowns in South Dakota. This section contains histories of these Wyoming locations.

CAMBRIA (Coal Mine)

Just south of the Cambria salt operation was a large coal-mining town with the same name. The coal town of Cambria was founded in 1887; it shut down in 1928 when the coal vein pinched out. At its peak in 1904, the mine employed 550 men, and the town boasted a population of 1,400. Kilpatrick Brothers & Collins, contractors to the

The Black Hills of Wyoming is a place with an unforgiving environment, stark beauty, and sparse population.

railroad, built the town and operated the mines. This was a company town. The coal was used by the Chicago, Burlington and Quincy Railroad as fuel for their steam locomotives. There was a large company commissary store where the miners could pay for things with company scrip and other locals could shop with cash. The developers also built a reservoir, bank, courthouse, train depot, opera house, school, lodge hall, recreation hall, a two-story hotel, two churches, numerous company offices, and more than 150 miners' homes. Since Cambria was a company town, there were no saloons or dance halls. The men went to Newcastle for these distractions.

The mine closed at the end of the final day's work shift and the town emptied literally overnight. (I was very fortunate to meet a nice lady whose father blew the work whistle that day. I met her during breakfast at a nice family café in Newcastle. Locals in these communities have a wealth of historical knowledge and are often eager to share it with you—not unusual in most of Wyoming.) During World War II, most of the town was dismantled. Still, many structures remained standing in the 1970s, which is amazing because this was a place built of wood and surrounded by pine forest—the perfect combination for fire to do its work.

After the mines closed, the site was used little. The post office stayed open only until December 31, 1928. The Farm Security Administration, a New Deal program, occupied one of the abandoned buildings during the 1930s. Local hunters and prospectors freely used the numerous vacant homes.

This is a much-photographed site. The Farm Security Administration took seventy-seven thousand photos from 1935 to 1942. The purpose of the photos was to show the poverty of farmers and migrant workers. Most of the photos were intentionally bleak in appearance.

Northeast of the town, there is a cemetery with many ornate tombstones. Area residents, including those in Newcastle, discourage visits to Cambria or almost any Black Hills ghost. They have had too much trouble with arson, theft, litter, trespassing, vandalism, etc. Too many tourists forget the simple rules: take nothing but pictures, leave nothing but footprints.

The coal town of Cambria is located just north of Newcastle, in a small valley up Cambria Creek. You must go through private property to access this site, and permission to pass through must be granted. You are discouraged from even asking. The site itself is also on private property, and again, permission must be arranged to visit. Locals say some buildings are still standing here, that others collapsed, but that most were moved. Coal waste is plentiful at the head of Cambria Canyon. The area's pine forest is still recovering.

CAMBRIA (Salt Mine)

A second ghost town named Cambria was a salt-mining operation. Salt was a very valuable commodity in the pioneer days of the Black Hills. It was used in bulk for many reasons, including for food or hide processing, to preserve food, for use in medicine, and most importantly, for mining. It was used to chloridize gold and silver ore.

In the beginning of the Black Hills mining rush, the nearest railroad was almost two hundred miles away. Freight costs for hauling even such a simple thing as salt were extremely high for the mines. When there is a market, business will try to provide. Europeans looked for and found salt springs at the head of Salt Creek Canyon on July 8, 1877. Salt Creek was already known in the area, and finding the springs was as simple as following the creek upstream. Even today, the white patches of chloride on the bottom of the canyon are easily visible to anyone.

In November 1878, James LeGraves came to the springs to start a salt-processing operation. During the next six years, LeGraves produced salt during the summer months by simple means of evaporation. Most of the salt went to the mines, but some went to the general stores in the towns of Deadwood and Lead.

This is all that remains of the Cambria salt extraction mine.

In 1904, N. H. Darton issued a promising report stating that the spring here discharged about thirty-five thousand pounds of salt a day. The water discharge is a little more than 5 percent salt in content. Even with an expanded rail network, the western markets still needed Cambria's salt. In 1907, an investment group, encouraged by the Darton report, committed a large amount of capital to expand the salt operation. It was known as the Cambria Salt Company. Brine was pumped about ten miles west to an evaporating and purifying plant near the Cambria Coal Mines. Coal from the Cambria mines was used to fuel the plant; this is one reason for confusion over Cambria's location. (Many sources have given an incorrect location for either the coal or salt operations.) The company unsuccessfully attempted to locate the bed of rock salt from which the brine discharged. At least three wells were drilled, with one as deep as 825 feet. The wells can still be seen here today. The operation was a failure, and the equipment of the Cambria Salt Company was sold at a public bankruptcy sale on May 11, 1909. This ended the "salt" history of Cambria. In addition to the wells, the only other remains here are a historical marker, an old wagon road, piping, and some debris.

INYAN KARA (Crook)

This is a mixed site (a site used for many purposes) that I stumbled upon on a pass-through. The area is bisected by State Highway 585 and is near the midpoint between the towns of Sundance and Four Corners. It is on the western edge of the Black Hills. This was a scattered farming and ranching community. As such, the remains are also widely scattered through the valley.

As you approach from the north, there is a historical marker on the west side of the road. This marker commemorates one of the first country churches in Wyoming and maybe the first permanent one in the valley. The Inyan Kara Methodist Episcopal Church was built by Reverend D. B. Chassell and citizens of the Inyan Kara community in 1891. The old church site is one mile west of the marker. A look through the binoculars showed no remains on the distant horizon.

A few miles south and on the east side of State Highway 585 are the Inyan Kara cemetery and a single abandoned building, which appears to be a one-room schoolhouse but could be the old Inyan Kara church. It has no steeple or any other signs relating to religion, but it does resemble the building etched into the historical marker north of here and could have been moved to this spot. The building is of clapboard construction with a stovepipe protruding from the center of its small roof.

Farther south on this highway and on the other side of the road is a boarded-up twentieth-century farming residence. More than a half dozen old frame or log structures surround this house. It is obvious that these buildings were constructed at a much earlier date than was the central house. Immediately behind this group are an additional four or five collapsed log structures. It must have been more than just a grouping of ranch sheds. There is one more standing log structure just a couple of hundred yards north of these buildings. All of these are vacant. The shadow of an old roadbed runs through the location and heads west. This was the old trail,

Top: This historical marker rests on the side of Wyoming Highway 585.

Bottom: This is the second church of Inyan Kara. A cemetery is adjacent to it.

Top: The site of the Inyan Kara settlement.

Bottom: There are various construction and building types here, indicating occupation over a long period of time.

which leads to Inyan Kara Mountain. This place was the actual old town site of Inyan Kara itself, and it is easy to see that it has been reoccupied several times—not as a town but as a ranch and farm. Other abandoned farms and ranches dot the landscape of the valley.

Most of these buildings appear to have been built at the same time, as well as vacated at the same time, but twice; that is, you will see structures made of logs all at the same stage of decay. Then there are newer buildings of modern construction with peeling paint. It is as if the valley was settled twice and abandoned twice.

The name's origin is Native American, but over time it has been misinterpreted, mispronounced, and misspelled by white settlers. The creek that runs by the town and a mountain that overlooks the area bear the same name. The word Inyan means "stone" in

Top: These are the remains of a horse-drawn sled.

Bottom: This site has been repeatedly used as a ranch.

the Dakota Sioux language, but the meaning of Kara has been lost in time. It is most likely a corruption of some other word or words. Some claim it was the word Kaga meaning "to make," "to cause," or "to form." It is further said that the Sioux called the mountain Inyan Kaga Paha (the third word, Paha, means peak). This would make the name "stone made peak." Since the mountain is made of broken volcanic rock, this makes sense.

This was probably also the site of Camp Bradley, the fourth base camp of Professor Walter P. Jenney's 1875 expedition. This was a government expedition sanctioned by the Department of the Interior for the purpose of assessing the potential for land development in the Black Hills. The land had not yet been purchased from the Indians, but the department was confident the matter would be resolved to the government's liking.

General Custer also traversed the valley during his 1874 Black Hills expedition. These were not the first two white expeditions to the Black Hills; they were not even the first two expeditions to Inyan Kara, but they were probably the most important. The Custer party climbed the summit and while there, chiseled "74 Custer" into the rock. Some say it is still there as a ghostly reminder of our not-too-distant past. Farther south on the highway, a historical marker commemorates this. There is some controversy over exactly what was carved, as sources disagree with each other. One source says the rock carving stated "GAC US 7th." A photo in one book shows "G.C. U.S. 7," but the photo is uncaptioned and Custer was known to leave his carved initials on a number of locations in the Hills. A magazine article from 1971 goes as far as to state that these initials have disappeared. The Forest Service was unusually vague and unhelpful when I inquired about the carving. This was due to their concerns over protecting such historic sites from the constant scourge of vandalism.

The stone foundations and collapsed remains of older structures are scattered around the site.

This is a place of wind and waves of gently swaying grass. It makes you feel that, if you were to listen carefully, you could almost hear the faint call of a bugle just over the next ridge melodically playing "Gary Owen."

MINERAL HILL (Crook)

The information for this location came from one book and two websites. All three sources were word-for-word identical. The websites probably copied the book whose information dates to 1974. Maps were the only additional information source I used before I made my visit.

This twentieth-century construction was an Inyan Kara ranch home.

Mineral Hill was an on-and-off gold-mining operation that dates back to the 1880s. In 1904, there was a large twenty-stamp mill in the town of Welcome that processed the large amount of ore from Mineral Hill. This location is about a half-mile northwest of Welcome and two miles southwest of Tinton. It is bisected by Spotted Tail Creek. These three towns are all remote locations situated within a maze of rough roads. They are on private property, posted, and locals discourage visitors. Winter or bad weather can make roads impassable. A topographic map and the ability to use it are required. The Forest Service owns the Mineral Hill fire tower on nearby Cement Ridge.

I found mostly debris on my visit. Numerous old small dams across both Sand and Spotted Tail creeks are easy to see. One dam formed a small millpond that I had seen in an old black-and-white photo. Cattails now grow in the remnants of these ponds, and all the dams were breached. The impounded water would have been used for panning and ore separation. The mill itself was now gone. All that remained were concrete foundations and lots of lumber. Homes varied from dugouts to log cabins and even to newer structures. Most of the older structures even appear to have been wired for

Right: All that remains of this mine building is its foundation.

Top: Collapsed miners' cabins and junked autos are scattered around Mineral Hill.

Bottom: For a miner, this wood-burning stove would have been a source of heat as well as a means for cooking.

electricity. (In many cases an obvious later addition.) The only other remains were junked autos, equipment, and prospecting trenches.

Another major gold strike occurred on nearby Negro Hill. The Hill got its name for the black miners who worked it. Originally, it was called a more derogatory term, but mapmakers have changed it to its modern name. In the frontier days, mining camps were heavily segregated. Western mining communities were divided into the "bad" and "good" sides of the tracks, and between miners who favored the Confederacy and those who favored the Union. Neighborhoods were even divided by European heritage, including Irish and German. Separate "China Towns" were common here. Indians were not allowed under any circumstances.

In the case of Negro Hill, these hardworking men mined the land closest to a major gold strike that they were allowed to mine. The land others had thought to be barren of minerals turned out to be rich in gold ore. In 1879, a group of black prospectors discovered a major ore body between Mineral Hill and Tinton. The gold ore from that location was sent to the mill at Mineral Hill. To my knowledge, there are no remains on Negro Hill.

Mineral Hill was once a company town. Old photos show a number of intact structures. Construction was done mostly with rough lumber so age had caught up with much of it. The mill itself was said to be intact and operating intermittently. The main mine is on the east side of Prospect Creek along with at least two others I found. The mine entrances are all collapsed.

Some sources claim that some or all of Mineral Hill is in South Dakota. This is not true; the entire site is in Wyoming. The road is very rough and should not be attempted in bad weather. A tax assessment notice posted on a tree showed the area is still panned for gold. Many other metals, particularly tin, have been mined in the area, and remains of such endeavors can be found scattered around.

The best time to visit is in summer. The site is beautiful for hiking.

MOSKEE (Crook)

Sources conflict over this site's location and physical status. It appears on all maps, including the official state highway map, as lying directly on a county road. Still, one website claims it is instead four miles up a private drive; it also claims there is a single standing building and that the rest of the location has been leveled by the Homestake Mining Company. Another describes this location as a community of eight houses on Cold Springs Creek. There may be two locations with the same name, or this may be a mine or sawmill and the town that serviced the work site. Other books and websites claim there is much more to this location. Either the information is old or there were two different locations.

I found Moskee simply by using the state highway map. The northern approach off I-90 down the Black Hills Grand Canyon is a very scenic route. Upon my arrival to Moskee, I noticed a sign stating that the southern approach was closed. The sign did not give a reason for the Forest Service road closure and it did not say by whom or at what time it may reopen. Kinda takes the meaning out of the word "service."

Old mine shafts like this one dot Mineral Hill.

Above: This was the largest mine at Mineral Hill. The entrance has collapsed, but mineral-stained water still leaches out from it.

Right: This is the only house in the town of Moskee.

Moskee got its start in the early 1900s as a lumber and sawmill town. How and when the town got its current name is subject to conjecture. It was also known as (in probable order): Bearsville, Homestake Wyoming Camp, and Laviere. When the town applied for a post office in 1925, it did so under the name Laviere. It was rejected and resubmitted under the name Moskee. The Postal Department explained that the first name was too much like other Wyoming towns; Moskee was accepted.

Lumber cut in Moskee was mostly milled into railroad ties by the McLaughlin Tie Company, which closed operations in 1907. A small cottage community continued here until 1921 when the Homestake Mining Company took over the area. Homestake developed the town extensively into a lumbering and sawmilling company town to provide timbers for its mine. The logs, lumber, and mine timbers were hauled out by heavy trucks, which often used an old road built by the McLaughlin Tie Company during the early 1900s. Homestake built a sawmill, a large boardinghouse for loggers, a washhouse, a long maintenance building with boiler room and shops, at least a half dozen houses, and a very large gravity-fed water tank. The tank got its water from a nearby spring and provided water for both the town and its fire hydrants. The hydrants had sheds built over them to keep

This is one of a remaining handful of still-intact snow sheds that cover fire hydrants in Moskee.

them snow-free during the winters. Between the pine forest, frame buildings, and the sawmill, the threat of fire was always greatly feared.

The town grew slowly; the post office was added in 1925 and a school in 1928. At about this time, the company provided the town with its own electric generating plant. At its peak in the 1930s, there were about two hundred people. During WWII, the mill and company town were closed and never reopened. After that, the town was occasionally used by local hunters.

When you arrive in Moskee, your first question will be, "Is this it?" Your next question will be, "Why is this place on the state highway map?" While this is beautiful country, there is not really a town here. There is one house with "Moskee Wyoming" in raised metal letters on its front; it was probably just a hunting cabin. The large water tank is still standing on the hill overlooking the town site. The water tank is constructed of wood and still completely intact. Its water flume lies strewn on the ground below. Three sheds that probably covered the town's fire hydrants also remain. In certain places, there are water valves at ground level with wooden boxes built around them. Other than that, the only other remains are scattered debris, piping, or boards. Today, the area is still used for hunting and logging.

To reach Moskee from the north, take I-90 to exit 191 and head south on Moskee Road for about twelve miles. This road runs through the town site. From the south, take U.S. Highway 85 and turn onto Forest Road 807 near the Hardy Ranger Station, which is a good place to ask for directions. This is also a good place to see if the southern approach is even open. Check road and fire conditions or ask any other pertinent questions. Forest Road 807 ends as a "T" intersection at Road 207. Turn right and Moskee should appear immediately.

While Moskee is in the Black Hills, it is not within the boundaries of the National Forest. Remember, this is private property—treat it as such.

TINTON (Crook)

This town is located on the South Dakota–Wyoming state border, with the borderline supposedly running up and down Main Street. (Websites show a photo of a grass-covered street with frame buildings on both sides and claim this is Main Street. The trouble is that this street runs east-west and the South Dakota–Wyoming border runs north–south.) National Forest Road 222, from which you can view the town, was the main road that divided the town between the two states. Today, most, if not all, buildings on the Wyoming side have been replaced by the latest mining operation. The blacksmith shop, post office, school, hotel, and other parts of the town's business section were on this side. The old mill, shaft house, and numerous mine buildings from the tin boom days elbowed right up to the site. This part of town was demolished in 1996. Tinton is still a photographer's dream and probably the best ghost town in the Black Hills.

Tinton got its start as a placer gold-mining town in 1876, but the ore deposits were not extensive and were soon exhausted. At that point, the community probably was not called Tinton; whatever the name may have been has been lost to history. Tinton almost faded from existence, but the Black Hills tin rush revived it. People

Top: This water tank was fed by a spring. It was part of the town's firefighting system.

Bottom: The view from the Moskee water tank. The field below used to be full of rows of stacked logs waiting for shipment.

Some of the buildings were businesses, but most were miners' homes.

had known there was placer tin in the area since 1876; in 1884, a hard-rock tin strike was made. This was a boomer, and by 1904, a company-type town had been built by the Tinton Company. Most of the buildings there now are from this period. At its peak, Tinton's business section included a bunkhouse, boardinghouse, hotel, bank, blacksmith shop, post office, grocery, company store, school, miners' hall, newspaper, and more. Also, there were many mine structures and plenty of housing.

During its tin production phase, Tinton became the "classic" company mining town. It was owned by many different mining companies, including the Boston Tin Company, the American Tin Plate Company, the Tinton Company, and the Tinton Reduction Company. These companies not only ran the town, they were the town. It is still the same way today, down to the company store.

The mine closed down during the early 1930s, but it was partially replaced by a sawmill. The town also had an operating school and a general store. The school had two rooms and housed eight grades. Mining activity picked up just before WWII when the U.S. government conducted a mineral survey. A lot of test drilling and tunneling was done for the survey, which revealed a list of rock minerals in various quantities. These included amblygonite, columbite, and tantalite; the latter is mined there today.

This building has a sheltered front entrance to protect against the Hills' harsh winters.

During WWII, the tin mining resumed here and continued periodically until the 1950s. Most wartime mining production at Tinton centered on the Feldspar and Lithium mines. All of these mining operations failed to show a profit. Historically, mining operations (except the present one) at Tinton have been conducted at a financial loss.

Most sources claim that today, the town consists of a miners' hall, a post office, a store with a company sign, and about ten homes lining both sides of Main Street. I cannot confirm all of this; on my visit, there was no one to question. Much of the area was posted and hence, off limits. Still, there was much to see. Mining structures and debris occupy a lot of area around town. Many more houses are downhill and out of sight from the road. The housing stock is mixed. Many homes belonged to miners. These were done with frame and tarpaper construction. Some were even constructed with rough-hewn lumber. Other homes had plastered walls and shingled roofs and obviously belonged to management, supervisors, and owners at one time. Some of these houses even had sidewalks; a few were wood, others concrete. These homes even had brick fireplaces, whereas others only had stoves with a stovepipe stack. One building had a concrete core at its center; this may have been a bank vault or cold storage for a grocer or butcher.

The house, while bigger than most others in Tinton, was built using cheap tarpaper.

A fallen tree had heavily damaged a house just east of Tinton. The story is that some loggers felled the tree onto the structure for the fun. Supposedly, this was a house for "soiled doves" otherwise known as prostitutes. Miners would have to leave a company town like Tinton to obtain certain services.

Getting to Tinton requires a topographic map and a good vehicle or the will to take a long hike. Any route you choose will go through very scenic and rugged country. The best way to drive in is from the South Dakota side on National Forest Road 222. According to the route you take and the source you use, there are several ghost towns along the way. An often-suggested route lies at the very back of Spearfish Canyon. It proceeds for six miles west of Iron Creek. In the winter, any of these roads may be snowed in.

Time forgot about Tinton for a while. By about 1940, local hunters were using it as a spot to hunt deer. Today, the town is fenced and posted. The photos of Tinton that appear on the Internet are taken from the road that runs through the site.

The current property owner is commercial miner Tinton Enterprises. It is currently mining a mineral called tantalum. Tantalum is a refractory metal with many uses, including use in nuclear weapons components. Supposedly, the material being mined here is used to make dinner china. The company mines seasonally. In the winter, they work around Deadwood. During the summer, the Tinton operation is worked.

The site is basically divided in half: the Wyoming half has the past and current mining operations, while the South Dakota half has most of the buildings that you see posted on websites. In the center of this and out of sight from the road is Roosevelt Square. It's been said that Kermit Roosevelt, son of Teddy, spent the winter of 1920 in Tinton. The local residents named the square "Roosevelt" in his honor. There are probably between thirty and forty buildings in this half of town, including the ones that collapsed.

Locals pronounce this place Tint-In and correct you if you do not pronounce it as such. Some of the information included in this section was obtained from a man who wandered into my camp. He claims he was Tinton's winter caretaker for thirteen years.

A few miles southwest of Tinton, in Crook County, Wyoming, are Mineral and Welcome, two more ghost town locations.

TUBB TOWN/FIELD CITY (Weston)

Slightly east of Newcastle and the junction of U.S. Highways 85 and 16 are the ruins of Tubb Town. It is one of eight Wyoming Black Hills ghost towns. Tubb Town was an attempt at a railroad town on the western edge of the Black Hills that got started in the spring of 1889. It was a modest beginning. DeLoss Tubbs of Custer, South Dakota, built and operated a store. This place was named Field City by Tubbs but called Tubb Town by everyone else. The town was built on the gamble that the railroad would choose this area for its next line. The town was said to have few laws and many saloons. Like many other western locations, Tubb Town claims Calamity Jane as a visitor. She was known to have lived and worked in the Black Hills at this time, so there may be something to this claim.

The discovery of coal at Cambria enabled the Burlington and Missouri River Railroad to come farther west. Tubbs and other businessmen became "boomers" and laid out Field City along Salt Creek. The city's backers asked far too high a land price, and in November, the railroad rerouted two miles farther west. This made Newcastle a boomtown and Field City a stillbirth. The residents quickly gave up the ghost and moved to Newcastle, taking even their buildings with them. Tubb Town was born and died in the same year.

Since residents took their buildings with them, one may wonder why Tubb Town appears on numerous maps and atlases as a ghost town location. There are two reasons for this. First, there is a Wyoming historical marker dedicated to Field City at the original site along Highway 16. Second, there was an attempt to create a tourist ghost town, and its remains are located here.

Al Smith, founder of the "Accidental Oil" operation, attempted a tourist attraction just west of the historical marker. He bought buildings from Newcastle. These were disassembled and moved to tourist Tubb Town. The endeavor was not a success. Most of the buildings are from the 1920s. Two still remain on private property on the north side of Highway 16. More buildings are kept in the back storage lot of Accidental Oil. Some lay as stacks of lumber. They had been disassembled but, like "Humpty Dumpty," never put back together again. One structure appears to have been a sheepherder's wagon.

Intended for Tubb Town, this tattered shepherd's wagon sits in the open-air museum of Accidental Oil.

Ironically, this is actually the old location of Tubb Town. Permission to enter may be obtained at the Visitor's Center of nearby Accidental Oil, also a point of interest. Tubb Town is located on the northern side of Highway 16, 7.9 miles west of the South Dakota–Wyoming border.

WELCOME (Crook)

The welcome mat is not out in Welcome, a town located in a very remote and beautiful part of the Black Hills National Forest.

This field is the location of original Tubb Town. The two buildings were moved here from Newcastle.

Arsonists, litterbugs, souvenir hunters, thieves and vandals have made others feel unwelcome in parts of the Black Hills, including this town.

The ironic thing is so many books use it as a point of reference. If these books send you to Tinton, Mineral, and others, they send you via Welcome. Some even suggest you ask for directions here. Good luck—there is usually no one to ask. Also, Welcome is only on limited National Forest maps.

Its history is sketchy. It was a service mining town during both the gold and tin rushes. In 1904, the Golden Empire Mining Company built a twenty-stamp mill here to serve the gold mines of Mineral Hill. The Black Hills Tin Company also ran some operations here at one time.

Welcome is situated along Sand Creek. The remains consist of one intact two-story log residence, the ruins of three others, an old pump house, and an ore cart. There was a National Forest sign that said, "Welcome," but on my last visit it was missing. Souvenir hunters had most likely stolen it. The owners of the only occupied residence in Welcome were hoping the Forest Service would replace it. The residence was recently rebuilt. The building had to be lifted so that a foundation could be placed underneath it. The house had been built so well that the shell had outlasted the original wood and stone floor joists. It was built by German carpenters who obviously knew their work. There is a 1920s shed behind the house; the ore cart is in the front yard.

In town, a dog charged at me; it turned out to be a friendly charge. The dog's name was Rose, and she accompanied me to the next ghost town of Mineral Hill. She was a very nice mid-afternoon companion, even stopping with me during a lunch break.

Sources have their preferred routes to this site. All agree that whichever route you take, it is a hard travel. Tinton, Mineral Hill, and the South Dakota border are all within a couple of miles. The best time to visit is the summer; winter or bad weather can make roads impassable. To find Welcome, you will need the correct topographic or National Forest map and the ability to follow them.

Be aware—the National Forest map has some inaccuracies. It shows a road passing in front of Welcome; it no longer does. Now there is a fence and a small pond where the map says there is a road. Instead, there is a road that goes around and behind Welcome on its approach to Mineral Hill; this road is not on the map. On your way to and at Mineral Hill, you will see more roads and trails that are also not marked on the National Forest map. This is a good and very useful map, but do not consider it to be flawless. Such thinking about any map can get you into a lot of trouble. Again, weather can enter into things. Lack of visibility can keep you from seeing important terrain features. The morning I started this hike, the fog kept visibility at about twenty feet. I stuck to the roads and the sun burnt off the morning mist by about nine o'clock.

If you are fortunate enough to meet the only family in Welcome, be nice to them because they are nice people. They had a wealth of information and directions and were also Rose's owners. They were nice enough to tell me which set of boards on the ground was the old post office. I was even treated to a viewing of a scrapbook on the history of the area.

Top: This house is the last standing building at Welcome that is occupied. It has a large "W" on its chimney.

Bottom: These disassembled buildings were to be reassembled for use at "tourist" Tubb Town. They originally came from Newcastle.

SOUTH DAKOTA

railroad ghost towns

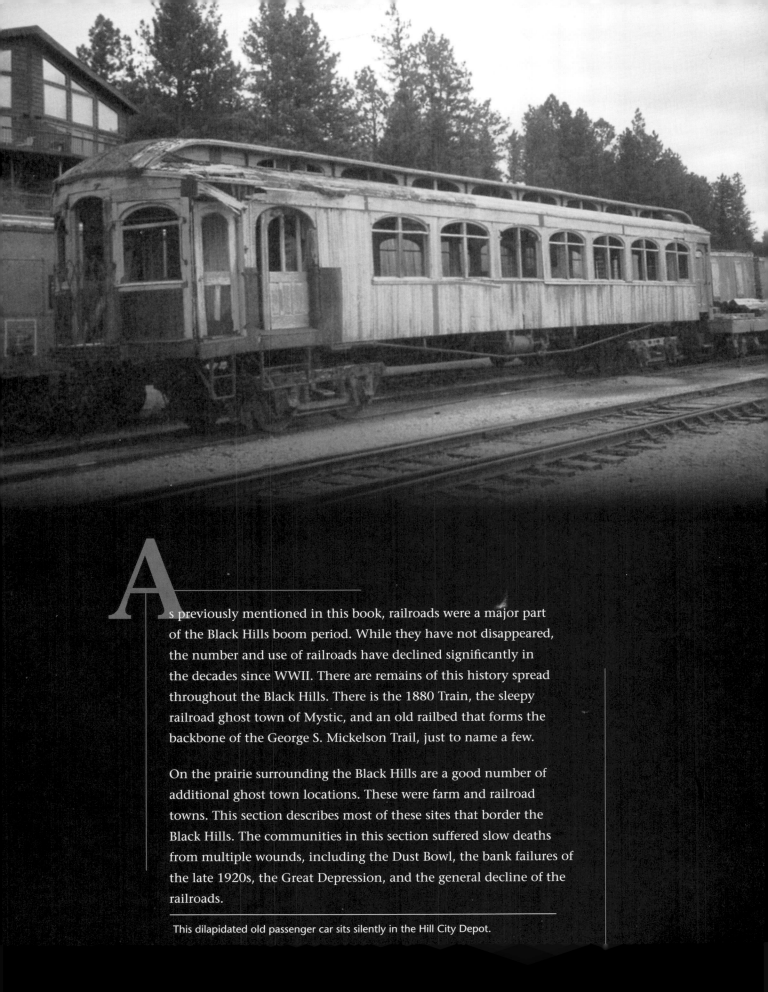

As previously mentioned in this book, railroads were a major part of the Black Hills boom period. While they have not disappeared, the number and use of railroads have declined significantly in the decades since WWII. There are remains of this history spread throughout the Black Hills. There is the 1880 Train, the sleepy railroad ghost town of Mystic, and an old railbed that forms the backbone of the George S. Mickelson Trail, just to name a few.

On the prairie surrounding the Black Hills are a good number of additional ghost town locations. These were farm and railroad towns. This section describes most of these sites that border the Black Hills. The communities in this section suffered slow deaths from multiple wounds, including the Dust Bowl, the bank failures of the late 1920s, the Great Depression, and the general decline of the railroads.

This dilapidated old passenger car sits silently in the Hill City Depot.

Entry into these Ardmore buildings is unadvised—the floor joists have been stolen.

These towns served the rail lines that served the Black Hills.

ARDMORE (Fall River County)

At the time this was written, Ardmore was probably the best and most complete ghost town standing in South Dakota. Ardmore was born in 1889 as a railroad town with bad water. The wellwater here was fine for steam engines but unfit to drink. Drinking water was hauled in by railroad. When the train stopped in town, the women of the community would come running with milk cans to use as water containers. When the railroad no longer stopped in Ardmore, the town lost its water source. The town had a municipal water tower that still stands today, but its water was unfit for human consumption. It provided water pressure and was used to flush toilets, wash cars, pressure the town's fire hydrants, water lawns, clean clothes, but not a drop for drinking.

Downtown Ardmore, the structure at the far left, was the first business building in town. It was the Land Office and later became a bank.

The American Legion Post was the site of numerous weekend dances.

Dora Moore was the first teacher here; it is claimed that the town is named for her, but that has been disputed. The town's one claim to fame is that President Calvin Coolidge once had lunch here during a town picnic put on by the local Farm Bureau office. A picture of the event hangs in the Game Lodge in Custer State Park; the date was July 4, 1925.

Ardmore became a service center for a large farming community. There was a bank, hotel, small department store, garage, and more. Dances were held regularly at the American Legion Post. The rural population shrunk drastically with the Dust Bowl and Great Depression. The town was already a mere shadow of its old self when the railroad put in the final nail. Today, the town is bedeviled by squatters and vandals.

Ardmore is easy to find; its location is shown on all appropriate maps, including the official state highway map. The town is in the extreme southwest corner of South Dakota on State Highway 71. The town is not totally vacant; there is a year-round population of two. One family still holds its annual reunion here.

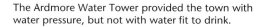

The Ardmore Water Tower provided the town with water pressure, but not with water fit to drink.

Top: The long two-story building was built as either a hotel or a railroad worker's boardinghouse. Today, it serves as a part-time private residence and is used for an annual family reunion.

Right: A business building next to the railroad tracks has lost its name twice. The name has faded from the false front and is completely gone from the roof's electrically lighted sign.

Top: Abandoned autos and antiquated farm equipment litter the town.

Middle: A highway maintenance garage that has fallen out of use.

Bottom: At its prime, Ardmore had good housing. This nice frame home had a bay window and an enclosed front porch.

Below: Concrete sidewalks indicate a community of some prosperity.

Top: Buffalo Gap has numerous vacant false-front businesses.

Bottom: In Buffalo Gap, many of the buildings, such as this bank, were built of native pink sandstone.

Right: The streets of Buffalo Gap are lined with so many boarded-up, false-front business buildings that it looks like a Hollywood movie set.

BUFFALO GAP (Custer)

This was a true boomtown. With the Black Hills to the north and the Cheyenne River to the south, this location formed a geological gap through which buffalo herds funneled through, hence the name Buffalo Gap.

Beaver Creek flows into the Cheyenne River here. The buffalo herds used the Beaver Creek Basin to move back and forth from the hills to the prairie. Great land for buffalo is also great land for cattle, and cattlemen rushed to the area.

The community got its start as a stage station for freight and passengers in the late 1870s. When the Chicago and Northwestern Railroad came through in 1885, a town sprung up in the middle of this semi-pass and took the geological feature's name for its own.

At the time, South Dakota was still a territory, and the mining and timber booms continued in the Black Hills. The railroads rushed rail lines to the area to get their share of the business and wealth that

Left: Notice the hand-carved support pillars holding up the porch roof.

Top: In the last century, Buffalo Gap has had at least three firehouses; these two are no longer in use.

Bottom: This firehouse in Buffalo Gap is still operating.

came with it. The business at Buffalo Gap was cattle, and business was good.

Between the cattle hands and railway workers, the town was bustling with activity. It is claimed that, at its peak, there were forty-eight saloons and gentlemen's clubs in town. Many other businesses like banks, hotels, restaurants, and more sprang up. Some still stand today. A few were built of local sandstone. These are beautiful buildings that attest to the town's past wealth. The wealth left due to all the usual suspects: the Dust Bowl, the Great Depression, loss of rural population, and the decline of the railroads.

Today, the town has a population of 164, but there are so many vacant business buildings that the place looks like a Hollywood film set. There are three fire departments, but only one is still in use. False fronts, grass-covered sidewalks, and rusting fire hydrants are all common. Old banks, hotels, saloons, and other businesses still stand from the boom days. Alongside railroad tracks are vacant farm and grain business buildings. These structures were built much recently. The entire community is a shutterbug's dream.

At one time, this was probably a hotel or dance hall, both of which abounded in Buffalo Gap.

Buffalo Gap is located about one mile east of State Highway 79 on County Road 2. This is a paved, all-weather road. The town of Oral lies to the south and Fairburn is to the north. There are few services here. The community is marked on all appropriate maps and atlases.

BURDOCK (Fall River)
SITE NOT VISITED

Located on the western edge of the Black Hills is the site of Burdock. It was started as a CB&Q railroad town and was originally called Argentine. Later, the community survived as a small gas stop and service center for local farmers and ranchers. There was a school, post office, and combination gas station/grocery store, along with a few homes. Trains no longer stop here; neither does anything else. Today, Burdock sits on County Road 769 in extreme northwest Fall River County. The ghost town of Dewey is just north of here. Burdock has a prairie environment, so there is no shade but plenty of wind. According to the Parker and Lambert book and some websites, most of the buildings, while vacant, still stand intact and shuttered. Burdock appears on most maps and atlases of the area.

CONATA (Pennington)
SITE NOT VISITED

Conata was one of a string of railroad towns that began in 1907 when the Milwaukee Road Railroad pushed a line to Rapid City. Both the Dust Bowl and the Great Depression took a heavy toll on the town. When the railroad shut the line down on March 31, 1980, it was the final nail in the coffin.

According to several websites, remains here consist of a small number of railroad buildings, foundations, the railroad grade, and a reservoir that held water for steam locomotives. There are no residents, but there are rattlesnakes. It is located on a dirt road and has no services.

Some old businesses in Buffalo Gap have been rehabbed and converted into homes.

CRESTON (Pennington)
SITE NOT VISITED

Creston was born in 1907 as a railroad section town for the Milwaukee Road Railroad. The Dust Bowl, the Great Depression, and the decline of railroads after WWII caused the town to shrink drastically; the abandonment of the railroad line in 1980 killed the town.

The site is located on the banks of Rapid Creek, which at one time would have supplied water for steam locomotives. There are no services or residents here. Remains consist of building foundations, debris, farm equipment, and an old railbed.

Creston is located on a dirt road (Creston Road) in a dry and harsh environment. You will need a detailed local map and dry weather for travel. Creston Road goes right through the old town site and is parallel to the old railroad grade.

DEWEY (Custer)
SITE NOT VISITED

This location was a ranch before CB&Q railroad arrived and created a place called Dewey. It boomed as a cattle-shipping center during the early 1900s. When the trucking industry took over most shipments of cattle, Dewey began a long decline. Today, a small population still lives here, but most structures are vacant. These include the church, post office and school. Even half the homes are empty. Many of the buildings are original and have false fronts.

Dewey is marked on all maps, is easy to find and sits astride a good road. It can be reached from U.S. Highway 85 in Wyoming, which lies to the west, or U.S. Highway 16 in South Dakota, which is north of Dewey. The route running south from Highway 16 and through Tepee Canyon is the most scenic. The Burlington Northern still rolls through the town and has a few storage sheds along its right-of-way.

Some reports claim this town was named for Admiral Dewey after the battle of Manila, but this is unconfirmed. Dewey's elevation is 3,704 feet; this is average for the old railroad towns surrounding the Black Hills, so altitude should not be a problem. Carry extra water. There are no services in Dewey, and the entire area is very sparsely populated.

FAIRBURN (Custer)

This community started in 1886 as a railroad town on the Fremont, Elkhorn and Missouri Valley Railroad. The Chicago and North Western Railroad ran a line to the town from Buffalo Gap. It also served as the terminus for the short Warren-Lamb Lumber Company rail line. This brought timber from logging operations in what is now Custer State Park.

French Creek was the water source for the railroads' steam locomotives at Fairburn. The town is still there today, but trains have not stopped there in decades. There is a population of about sixty, served by a post office and a tiny school. The old business district contains some boom-period buildings, including a gas station, a

Top: This was probably one of Fairburn's many boardinghouses or hotels.

Bottom: This Fairburn hotel had been converted into a residence at one time. The sign above the porch says "Johnnie's Cocktails." On my visit, it appeared to be out of use.

Left: This was probably one of several Fairburn hotels. Most of their business came from the railroad passengers and workers.

Right: Looking north on Fairburn's Main Street towards the railroad tracks. One false-front business remains.

Top: I believe this Fairburn firehouse is out of service.

Bottom: All that remains of this Fairburn bank is its vault.

hall, two hotels, and more. Some buildings have false fronts. Ancient concrete sidewalks and bank vaults tell where other structures once stood.

Fairburn is marked on all appropriate maps and atlases and is easy to find. It is located about four miles east of State Highway 79 on a good all-weather road.

IMLAY (Pennington)

Imlay was one of several small railroad towns that popped up in 1907 on the Milwaukee Road Railroad's Murdo–Rapid City line. Today, it sits silently in a sea of sagebrush with prairie dogs and rattlesnakes as its only inhabitants. Like many others of its ilk, Imlay succumbed to the Dust Bowl, the Great Depression, the decline of the railroads, and being bypassed by highways. One difference from the other Murdo–Rapid City rail towns is that this site actually has a grove of trees. The town residents planted these trees here to serve as shade and a windbreak. Other remains include the old railroad bed, debris, and a small number of standing buildings. This includes the old railroad depot from nearby Interior, South Dakota, another town that has disappeared over time.

This place is fire-hot in the summer and subject to blizzard conditions in winter—do not visit at those times. The best time to visit is during a dry spring or fall day. Imlay is marked on a number of older maps and atlases. It rests on a dirt road about a half-mile north of State Route 44. It is plainly visible from the highway. Most websites list this town as being located in Jackson County; this is incorrect.

ORAL (Fall River)

In 1885, when the Fremont, Elkhorn and Missouri Valley Railroad reached the Cheyenne River southeast of the Black Hills, progress on the line was stopped until a bridge was built across the stream. Immediately, a little community dedicated to working men's

Above: The post office is the last business still open in Oral.

Below: The town name of "Oral" appears above the door of a disused railroad shack.

This abandoned business stands adjacent to the railroad tracks at Oral.

A portion of Provo's business district.

entertainment popped up. It was called Pimptown for obvious reasons. As soon as the bridge was finished and its working crew moved on, so did Pimptown.

Later, a small railroad and farming town grew to occupy the same spot. Its name was Oral. The community is still there today, though smaller and quieter. The train still rolls through town but does not stop anymore. The post office is the only service here; all other businesses went out of business.

PROVO (Fall River)

Provo was born in the early 1900s as a railroad town for the Chicago, Burlington and Quincy Railroad. Luckily for Provo, just as the railroad business began to fade, the U.S. government opened the Black Hills Ordnance Depot only four miles to the west. This was a major boom for the town's economy. The post was open from early WWII to the early 1960s. When the post closed, Provo lost its economic life's blood.

Provo is marked on most maps and is easy to find. However, some maps confuse the communities of Igloo and Provo. Some local residents also use the names interchangeably; in fact, they are not interchangeable. Provo was off the post's east gate. Igloo is the community actually within the base. Unlike Igloo, Provo never grew to a large size. Children at Provo even went to school at neighboring Igloo. The road from the north is paved; from the south, it is gravel.

Derelict autos are Provo's most abundant commodity.

There is a small population of about twenty living in town, but most buildings are vacant. There are no services here. All businesses still standing are boarded up. There are a small number of original railroad boom-day buildings still intact. Most of these are being used as backyard sheds. The surrounding countryside is prairie.

Interestingly, there are a large number of derelict vehicles here. This is something I have encountered at a few other rural western ghosts such as Bosler, Wyoming, and Gem, Kansas. If you ask someone in town about these vehicles, you will get a vague answer, if any at all. When you ask elsewhere in the state, you sometimes hear wild but unsubstantiated rumors about them. For the curious, view all things from the road; this is private property—please respect it. Also, be on the lookout for rattlesnakes.

There are no services in Provo; all businesses closed shop long ago.

Above: One of the few buildings left in the isolated town of Rumford.

Right: This is State Road 471. On a nice weather day, it is a scenic pleasure drive; on a bad weather day, it can be a lonely nightmare.

RUMFORD (Fall River)

This was a railroad section town founded in 1889. Started by the Burlington Railroad as a simple depot and track siding, it was simply called "Siding No. 5." The company changed the site's name in 1894 to Rumford after it had grown into an actual town. The tracks are still in use but the town is not. The majority of what few buildings remain here are vacant. All construction is early to mid-twentieth century. Rumford appears on the state highway map, so the place is easy to find.

This is a prairie environment. That means cold winters and hot summers. Also, it is always windy. The land is very flat. The location is the very definition of isolated.

Rumford is eleven miles south of Provo on County Road 471. This is a gravel road. There are no services in town or along the route. The population is listed at fourteen, but a quick scan of the little community makes it evident that even this small number must be spread out over the surrounding prairie.

ST. ONGE (Lawrence)

French fur traders settled St. Onge long before the Black Hills gold rush. They obtained beaver pelts from the Hills through barter with the Indians there. The fur traders gave the town its name, and some claim that they left dates carved on wood beams in old buildings and in root cellars. On my visit to St. Onge, I could not find anyone who could show or tell me anything about these carvings. It is claimed these dates go back to the 1830s.

During the mid-1880s, the railroad came through, and the town experienced a second boom. During the early twentieth century, the town continued to grow as a farm community. Of course, the trade in beaver pelts had long since stopped being part of the community's economy. The railroad ceased making stops here in the 1990s. The rural farm population dropped significantly, and St. Onge has all but dried up.

There is a small population here; still, even half the housing is vacant. The old business district is totally abandoned, but several vacated business buildings attest to much better days. There is a pair of grand two-story sandstone structures. Other business buildings were built of brick, concrete, or lumber, and their construction spanned various time periods. Next to the train crossing there are a vacant farm business building and railroad siding. On the south side of town are an abandoned school and farm buildings.

St. Onge is located on State Highway 34 about seven miles northwest of I-90 at Whitewood and thirteen miles southeast of Belle Fourche. Services here consist of a gas station/convenience store with a pay phone. The location is shown on most maps and atlases, including the official State Highway Map of South Dakota.

Top: These fine sandstone structures are from the town's boom period and are located on Center Street.

Middle: This was once a fine hotel with a restaurant and bar.

Bottom: This abandoned farmhouse stands on the southern edge of town.

Top: Neither siding nor silo in St. Onge is in use.

Bottom: This is a St. Onge school that no longer hears the laughter of children. There is an interesting carving on the eve above the doorway.

Right: A church built in 1920.

SCENIC (Pennington)

Scenic isn't, but it is an interesting site with a lot to photograph. This is a twentieth-century ghost town located on State Highway 44 just off the western edge of Badlands National Park.

Its exact founding year is unknown to me. The Milwaukee Road Railroad gave the town an enormous boost in 1907 when its rail line came through, but some of the town's buildings predate this.

This town still has residents but also numerous abandoned buildings. Some of these structures are quite interesting. The Longhorn Saloon has a sign that proudly claims 1906 as a date of establishment; it also has a rack of animal skulls. There is an old school, a church, a motel, and more. More than half the homes are vacant in town. There is a combination food store/gas station and a second school here that is still in use. The old jail was built of rock and undressed stone cemented together. The steel bars of the prison cells are still in place.

Scenic is hot in the summer. It sits just off the south side of Highway 44 and is easy to locate on just about any map of South Dakota.

SMITHWICK (Fall River)
SITE NOT VISITED

Smithwick is a semi-ghost with a small population (listed at sixty-three) that started as a railroad town. During the boom days, railroads competed to bring service to the Black Hills. Just as their rail lines did, towns sprang up at regular intervals along the right-of-way. Some were workers' camps or "tie" towns. Others became water stops or railroad depots and had more staying power. When the railroads scaled back massively in the decades after WWII, many of these sites became ghost towns. This is Smithwick—it is still located on the state highway map and is just south of her sister ghost of Opal. The town was named after the Chicago and North Western Railway engineer who had been in charge of construction to that point. There are few, if any, services in Smithwick.

Top: This Scenic building's last function was that of a secondhand store.

Middle: This is the Longhorn Saloon in Scenic.

Bottom: This old stone structure was the Scenic jail.

Left: The Tatanka Trading Post. There are numerous businesses in Scenic, and most are closed.

OTHER

historical sites of the black hills

In addition to all of the ghost towns and national monuments, like Mount Rushmore in the Black Hills, there are other significant historical sites in the area worth a visit. This chapter contains the historical biographies for these sites. The places in this section are generally family-friendly, informative, photogenic, and easy to get to. A stop at any of them would be time well spent.

ACCIDENTAL OIL (Weston County)

This site is a museum and an unusual on-and-off oil operation, not a ghost town. There is a ghost town site (Tubb Town) next door, and some of its buildings are located on the museum's storage lot. It is approximately four miles east of Newcastle on the north side of State Highway 16. This tourist operation has narrated tours, on which you are led to the original hand-dug well. These tours are informative, an unchallenging walk, and

Pioneer cemeteries can provide historical data. These unusual markers can be found

This oil storage tank has been converted into a gift shop.

usually conducted by a member of the friendly Smith family. A small fee is charged for this service. Parking, the outdoor museum, and admission to the gift shop are free.

Its appearance is more of an abandoned oil operation than that of a museum. There is much old oil-drilling equipment here, some dating back to the 1880s. One drilling rig is from the infamous Teapot Dome. This is a great place to see the history of the oil industry in Wyoming. It covers a fair area at this location, and there is no shade.

This site's oil operation was much newer than most of the equipment on display here at the museum. The name Accidental Oil is a misnomer. This is a planned operation. The oil was found at a very shallow depth—a mere twenty-four feet. A lifelong oilman named Al Smith wildcatted this site in 1966. He leased the land from the government, and when he could not move a drilling rig onto the property before the lease ran out, he literally dug a well with a pick and shovel. After only a month of digging, he struck oil. The well's peak production, if indeed it could be called that, was five barrels of crude a day. This is not oil that can be refined; rather, it is an industrial-type lubricant. On my last visit, production was down to less than a barrel a day, and there was no buyer for the commodity.

Besides the museum of equipment, there is a viewing room so that one can see the seepage process by which this place operates. This is the actual well that Smith dug. There is also an unusual gift shop. The owners have converted a ten thousand-barrel, sixty-five–foot diameter, oil storage tank into their store. It is open daily from Memorial Day to Labor Day. The location is easy to find and offers convenient access on and off the highway. It is an informative and interesting stop. The remains of Tubb Town are virtually next-door.

Accidental Oil closed at the end of the 2006 season and has yet to reopen.

ANNA MILLER MUSEUM (Weston)

This is a great museum of the "Old West" located in Newcastle, Wyoming, which consists of a small collection of buildings covering the period from the 1870s through the 1930s. The main exhibits are housed in an old cavalry post, a rather long structure built with hand-hewn sandstone blocks; the blocks had been

Top: The open-air museum at Accidental Oil contains much antiquated historic oil field equipment. Some of it came from the infamous Teapot Dome oil reserve.

Bottom: At Accidental Oil, this was a steam-powered pump.

Left: This is the actual well Al Smith dug by hand.

cut from a quarry at nearby Salt Creek. It was built in the 1930s as a Works Progress Administration project and was the post for Company A, 115th Cavalry of the Wyoming National Guard—a rather late date for such military technology. The building used to contain the tack room, stables, and sergeants' quarters for the post. Today, the building contains a number of historical displays and is the centerpiece of the museum. Among the exhibits are dinosaur fossils, artifacts from the coal-mining ghost town of Cambria, and five different "period" rooms. Some of the Cambria exhibit had previously been located in the "Flying V" ranch resort. This was considered a fine display in itself when at the resort, but the collection was moved to Newcastle in about the year 2000.

Other buildings in the complex include a one-room schoolhouse, a frontier cabin, a stagecoach station, and an open country store. The school was called the Green Mountain Schoolhouse and is a typical structure of its kind from the period between 1890 and the 1930s. Inside, the school appears to be ready for morning class. It is in prime condition and contains many era items, such as a wood-burning stove, desks, blackboards, a globe, maps, and a lot more.

The stagecoach station is the Jenney Stockade cabin. It is reportedly the oldest building left from the Black Hills gold rush. It was used first as a cabin and later a stagecoach station on the Cheyenne Deadwood Trail.

This is the Anna Miller Museum. It was originally used by a cavalry unit in the Wyoming National Guard. (Courtesy of the Anna Miller Museum)

The museum, not surprisingly, is named after one Anna Cecelia (McMoran) Miller. She was the daughter of a local pioneer family and was a pioneer schoolteacher, school superintendent, and Newcastle's first librarian. Her husband was a sheriff named Billy Miller. He was killed in what was reportedly the area's last Indian battle.

The museum is located off U.S. Highway 16 in Newcastle, Wyoming, at 401 Delaware. It is open year-round with the exception of Sundays and charges no admission.

Its website is *http://www.newcastlewyo.com/anna.html*.

CAMBRIA CASINO (Weston)

An interesting and picturesque stop is the Cambria Casino, or as it is also called, the Flying V Guest Ranch. It was built for recreation and as a memorial to the coal miners of Cambria. Ironically, the resort was not completed until the mines closed.

The main lodge opened in 1928; the grand opening of the dance hall was not held until January 12, 1929. Construction had started in 1923, and the resort was opened in a piecemeal fashion, one building at a time. Miners did a good deal of the construction work. They used a large number of mine timbers for many things, among them to help construct the frame of the main lodge. Two pools were built: a fresh water pool supplied with water from Salt Creek and a hot salt water pool supplied with water piped from the Cambria salt springs two miles north of the resort.

The resort consisted of 2,280 acres donated by the Cambria Fuel Company. Up to seventy-five guests could be accommodated stylishly in the six cottages, which no longer exist, and in the main lodge. A museum was part of the original resort. It was in honor of Lewis T. Wolle, a company president for twelve years, and the miners who worked for him. Longtime drawing cards for this establishment, the memorial and its collection have been moved to the Anna Miller Museum in Newcastle, Wyoming. A dedication plaque is still embedded in an exterior wall of the lodge. The main physical structure at the resort is a large, two-story, sandstone lodge decorated in an English Tudor manner. The rock was hand-cut from a quarry just one mile away. There was also a casino, restaurant, meeting halls, a riding stable, and more.

When the coal company went out of business, the resort was leased to the Flying V Cattle Ranch. A large V, placed on a turret roof structure, is still there today. From 1936 to 1937, a room at the resort was leased out for use as a bar. From 1939 to 1949, the Flying V Guest Ranch was leased to the Reno Livestock Company. Later, the Flying V Guest Ranch operated as a bible camp and then a dude ranch before becoming a combination bed-and-breakfast and general restaurant. As this last business setup, it has gone through several owners. It operates today as a combination bed-and-breakfast, restaurant, and banquet hall for weddings, reunions, and such. As of November 18, 1980, it has been listed on the National Register of Historic Places. There are a small number of frontier-type buildings on the grounds, but they appear to have been moved there. The Flying V Guest Ranch, or Cambria Inn, is located a few miles northeast of "coal" Cambria. The Inn still does business there today on the east side of U.S. Highway 85, just north of Newcastle, Wyoming.

This was the Cambria Casino but today is the Flying V Cambria Inn.

CCC CAMPS (Various)

The three Cs stand for Civilian Conservation Corps. This program was established by Franklin D. Roosevelt as part of his alphabet-soup government response to the Great Depression. Under this program, employed men worked on projects in the National Forest and built parks—they did everything from building roads to helping fight forest fires to constructing lodges at parks. The workers lived military style in camps they built. In fact, the U.S. Army ran the camps. The program ran from 1933 until its termination by the start of WWII. A fair number of these camps were built in the Black Hills. A few were concentrated in the southeast corner of the Hills to construct Custer State Park.

There is one CCC camp with remains located within Custer State Park. This location is on French Creek, upstream from the Blue Bell Lodge. This was set up to help with the construction of Custer State Park. First, the workers set up a sawmill to make lumber. Then they built the camp in which they would live. This would be their eating and living quarters while they worked on other projects in the park. They continued to operate the sawmill to produce lumber for other structures in the park.

This is all that remains of the Mystic Camp.

There is not a lot to view here, but what makes it nice is how you view it—by horseback. You get your horse at the corral down the road a bit from the Blue Bell Lodge. The lodge, one of the original ones in the park, makes a wonderful lunch or dinner stop. The trail ride takes you up the creek and right through the camp. The remains of a couple of cabins and some machinery are scattered about. Cameras are not permitted, as their sounds may spook a horse.

When asked locally for a camp name, it was referred to as just the CCC Camp. It is possible that it was called French Creek Camp. The Parker and Lambert book lists a CCC Camp by the name of Camp Custer, and its description fits what I viewed from horseback on French Creek. However, the book does not say it is in Custer State

Park and gives coordinates west of the park for the Camp Custer location.

Another CCC camp location within Custer State Park was called Camp Narrows. This was a CCC Camp reportedly located at the Narrows on French Creek within Custer State Park. Some park literature showed it in this general area; it is also listed in the Parker and Lambert book as such. The site is located on a hiking/horse trail in a French Creek Natural area. There are probably no remains.

Most often all that is left is just a highway historical sign. The Mystic Camp in Pennington County has its original dedication marker. Easily visible on the west side of Forest Road 231, it is a crude, hand-carved gray slab. The field behind the marker was the location of the camp. The commemorative date inscribed in the stone is June 29, 1933. The camp operated until January 6, 1938, and at its peak, the camp had two hundred men. It is located about 5 1/2 miles south of the township of Mystic. Many additional old markers and historical plaques dot the Black Hills to reveal the locations of these bygone camps.

CENTRAL CITY (Lawrence)

Central City is not a true ghost town but is worth a visit for its number of historical and other interesting buildings. Located up Deadwood Gulch, this place is hemmed in a narrow valley. Deadwood Creek crowds the valley floor. This was the initial source for the town's gold and later would cause so many devastating floods. The confined environment led to dense construction and population patterns. This, in turn, led to frequent severe town fires.

The first gold prospectors started panning here in the spring of 1875. When they discovered placer deposits, miners' tents blossomed along with the spring flowers. The first permanent structure was built here in late 1875. By the fall of 1877, the gold rush had caused the town to mushroom into a far-flung community of ten thousand. At this time, Central City had sixteen mills, a church, newspaper,

This was a Central City firehouse during the boom period; today it is a private residence.

brewery, post office, telegraph office, and a school, which was the second one in the Black Hills. The first brick building built in the Hills was also here.

Central City acquired its name at a public meeting on January 20, 1877; this was the main purpose for the meeting. It is claimed that a man by the name of I. V. Skidmore, who had just come from Central City, Colorado, suggested the name.

This was an active, bustling, wealthy, and violent town. It rivaled Deadwood on this last level. Violence was frequent and often sudden. Sometimes, it was organized and even involved high explosives. Miners and mine owners had enough problems with each other, but mine owners would sometimes resort to extremes when dealing with their competitors. Often they would commit acts that today would be termed as unfair competitive practices—that is, they would set fire to or dynamite the competition's mine.

Real troubles hit Central City in 1883 in the way of a devastating flood. The town's location on Deadwood Creek acted as a funnel. The flood did heavy damage to the placer working, a couple of the mines, and a good portion of the business section. Another disaster struck this town on April 25, 1888, when a large fire destroyed a major portion of the community. The fire had started in a restaurant run by Lawrence Belleville. He had left the establishment for a short while to run an errand. On his return, he saw his place blazing in flames. Horrified, he turned, ran, and was never seen again. Most of the town was never rebuilt.

One more economic blow to the town came during the late 1880s when the water flume failed, and there was not enough capital to rebuild it. What was left of the community faded away with time. Photos as late as the Fourth of July celebration of 1990 show a fair number of two-story business buildings, a large crowd in the street, and the railroad still in operation here.

There are still many original buildings left like this church on Main Street.

This disused school crowds the floor of a small gulch.

Today, the population is less than two hundred, and the railroad tracks are gone. Most of what is left of the old town lies on the north side of the valley. A steep gully feeds into the north side of Deadwood Gulch, and a portion of Central City occupies it. A solid two-story school takes up the floor of this terrain feature and forces traffic to go around it. The school was opened in 1938, but the construction style is oppressive—it looks like a building from pre-WWII Berlin or Moscow. Many people of the day claimed the architectural style to be a beautiful proletarian view of the future. I think it makes buildings look like bunkers or air-raid shelters. Then again, at one time, this school did serve as the local civil defense shelter. The building was vacated as a school and put to other various uses over the years. It appeared to be out of use on my last visit, but it was the summer season, and there is not a lot of activity on most school properties at that time.

Most, but not all, of the housing stock is occupied in Central City. Many newer buildings rest on obviously older foundations. In other instances, that is all there is—a foundation. Many old buildings are in use; the old post office and City Hall still function. The C. G. & T. Hose Company building, an ancient frame firehouse, has been converted into a summer residence. It is still painted firehouse red and is complete with bell tower and hayloft. There is a small portion of the old main street with both open and vacant businesses, including the Central City Saloon and Central City Merchandise store.

Central City is easy to locate and reach. It sits between Lead and Deadwood on U.S. Highway 85. There are gas, food, and postal outlets.

FLAG MOUNTAIN OVERLOOK (Pennington)

This is a long abandoned mountain overlook in the Central Black Hills. The site is located on numerous Black Hills maps and is easy to find. The mountain is a few miles north of Deerfield Lake on National Forest Road 189. It is accessible via a short, but rough, dirt road spur. A sign simply stating "Flag Mt" marks the turnoff. The spur ends in a turnaround. A flight of roughly hewn stone steps leads from the turnaround to the overlook. Once on top of the lookout, you will be impressed by the stunning panoramic view. You will want binoculars and a camera with a wide-angle lens for this stop. Caution—there is a lightning strike hazard here. Children should be carefully supervised due to falling hazards.

This site lies in a state of extreme disrepair. Materials used to build it include concrete, small amounts of reinforcing steel, and white rock quarried onsite. Remains include a two-seat outhouse.

Top: Binoculars are great for day- or night-viewing here.

Bottom: The wooden structure at lower left is what remains of a restroom of sorts.

Left: The viewing platform at Flag Mountain Overlook.

This is a place I just stumbled across on a day's wandering. The Forest Service built the lookout, probably in the 1930s as a scenic tourist attraction.

GORDON STOCKADE (Custer)

These are the ruins of an authentic old western frontier fort, although it has been rebuilt at least twice: first in the 1920s, and then again in the 1930s by the Civilian Conservation Corps. On my last visit in 2004, it was closed due to danger of collapse. It is located about four miles east of Custer on U.S. Highway 16 at one of the entrances to Custer State Park.

Twenty-eight gold-hungry members of the Collins-Russell-Gordon party first built the stockade along French Creek in late December 1874. This determined band consisted of a boy, one woman named

These are the steps to the Overlook's dilapidated outhouse. Interestingly enough, it is a two-seater!

This replica was built on the site of the original stockade.

Annie D. Tallent, the group leader John D. Gordon, and twenty-five other men. This was the first large organized group of miners to establish themselves in the Black Hills; it was the beginning of the Black Hills gold rush. They had come from Sioux City, Iowa, and were determined to stay. A camp was set up. They then built a stout and fairly sizable stockade with bastions on all four corners. The fort was an eighty-foot square with ten-feet high walls, with bastions protruding out six feet. One shortcoming was that the firing loopholes were at shoulder-height and could have been used almost as well by attackers as by defenders. Inside the compound were three corrals, six or seven cabins, and a well.

Around the fort, these squatters laid out a town they called Harney City. They had hoped to get a jump on the gold rush and also to be the first boomers of the Black Hills. All of the construction was completed in only three weeks. After the construction, efforts turned to gold panning in the adjacent French Creek. Results were very disappointing, and the winter was proving harsher than expected. It was not long before discouragement set in and several members of the party left. Tallent wrote about the experience in a book entitled *Black Hills; or the Last Hunting Ground of the Dakotahs.*

This stockade contains copies of the original cabins. Due to the unsafe nature of the walls, the stockade is currently closed and fenced off.

The miners were there illegally, so the Army sent Captain John Mix and some Second Cavalry troopers to remove them. This was done in April 1875 with just four men and without firing a shot. With two former Gordon party members acting as scouts, Captain Mix and one other trooper entered the fort during a raging blizzard. The remaining eighteen squatters were removed to Fort Laramie without difficulty. Captain Mix said that if the party had resisted, he would have had to return to Fort Laramie for artillery. The captain's after-action report with accompanying diagram lists six cabins within the compound. Annie Tallent's book states there were seven and lists them by name.

The fort's first name came from one of the leaders of the expedition. The place has also been called Camp Harney, Fort Defiance, and Union Stockade. The latter was given in the summer of 1875 when General George Crook and his blue-clad troopers occupied the fort. In the fall, Captain Edwin Pollock was put in command and continued the Army's futile efforts to keep out illegal miners. With the onset of the gold rush, the post was soon vacated and had fallen into disrepair by the end of the century.

HARNEY PEAK (Pennington)

This is not the only abandoned Forest Service fire tower in the west, but it certainly is the best. Nestled atop the granite spires of the Black Hills is a gray stone ghost. The tower, rather than scarring the land, blends into the rock itself and, from a distance, appears at first to be just another granite spire. The CCC built the tower in 1939 for the Forest Service as a fire lookout. Local materials were used for economical reasons, but this also allowed the structure to blend into the peak. If you take the hike, you will appreciate the construction even more. All tools and materials were hauled in on mules or on someone's back. All construction was done by hand. A small dam and pump house were also built. The dam created a small reservoir on the peak, and this, along with the pump house, was used to generate electricity for the site. The structures are still there today, along with the tower, and all are listed as national historic landmarks.

On my first visit to the tower, there were no steps inside; on return trips, the Forest Service had installed new steps to restore access to the top. The panoramic view from the top of the tower is spectacular, if weather permits. A camera is a must—a wide-angle lens would work well. This is one of the gems of the Black Hills, only surpassed in majestic splendor by Mount Rushmore. The tower was constructed on Harney Peak, the highest point of the Black Hills. In fact, at 7,242 feet, this is the highest point (above the 20th parallel) between the Rocky Mountains in the U.S. and the Pyrenees Mountains in Western Europe. I cannot get over the fact that, at 7,200 feet, these are the Black Hills, and at 2,400 feet, the Ozarks are mountains. I pass this off to marketing.

The tower stands atop a stone pedestal. There are both internal and external staircases leading to the tower. The pedestal structure has its own exterior observation platform and contains a number of rooms built for the tower crew.

To reach Harney Peak, you must hike about three miles on one of two trails from any of three different trailheads. You should be in decent shape to attempt this slight adventure. The ascent from the Lake Sylvan Trailhead is twelve hundred feet. With the starting altitude of six thousand feet, you are above Denver, so beware of the possibility of altitude sickness. Take plenty of water and eat a light breakfast. Even though this is the highest point in the state, there is no "peak registration" book to sign. On the plus side, if you can tough out the six-mile hike, you can tell all of your friends you climbed a mountain and have the pictures too, again weather permitting. The weather reports you hear on your radio are for amusement purposes only. These reports are for cities sitting at three thousand feet on a treeless prairie and have little relevance in the hills at seven thousand feet, even when only twenty miles away. I have stood close to a campfire shivering in the snow while the radio claimed it was sunny and seventy-six degrees at the nearest town. A poncho in your pack is always a good idea on any mountain hike.

The only thing that can compete with the view from Harney Peak is the view of Harney Peak.

Left: Harney Peak's dam and firehouse were both hand-built. The reservoir still holds water.

Below: Been there, climbed that. This is the author standing on the Harney Peak powerhouse.

Most of the trailheads are in Custer State Park, another Black Hills treasure. One can obtain directions and trail maps here. The trails are all marked and coded by both number and color. My favorite is the No. 9 trail from Sylvan Lake. This lake is a most beautiful setting and makes for great photography. The very end of the hike is a steep ascent and involves quite a few steps, not including the ones in the tower.

A large number of postcards are produced for this attraction. They are usually aerial views of the locations and can be spellbinding. If you make the hike, you will find yourself buying them by the fistful.

There are a number of other towers located in the Black Hills; some are still in use. A good number are marked on various maps. Some, whether in use or not, are open to the public. One fine example is the Mount Coolidge Lookout in Custer State Park. It is still in use and open for public viewing. A forest fire came right up to its doorstep just a decade ago, and the land scars are still there.

IGLOO (Fall River)

Igloo was the name of a town that was not a town. You will find it on many older maps and atlases as a rural town at the end of a

road spur. This is a cold war deception and not a very good one at that. Every adult citizen in a three-state area knew Igloo was a local slang name for the Black Hills Ordnance Depot. The base was a huge three-sectioned complex that covered enough land for a fairly sizable county. More specifically, Igloo refers to the base contonement area. This is the part of a military base that contains the soldiers' housing and services like the post church, theater, service stations, and more—in other words, a small, self-contained city. The nickname of Igloo came from the shape of some of the ordnance bunkers used in the post's storage area. It was simply quicker and easier to say Igloo than Black Hills Ordnance Depot Contonement Area.

The base was built for and during WWII. The site mushroomed in size and was a beehive of activity at this time. The end of WWII led immediately to the start of the cold war, so the Black Hills Ordnance Depot was kept open to store and process various munitions. The processing was done at a second part of the post that was dedicated to the cleaning and packaging of military ordnance, including chemical weapons. It is rumored that other unconventional weapons were stored here, but this is unconfirmed. At this point, the name of Igloo was kept for security purposes.

A third and intentionally distant part of the post was for the storage ordnance, ammunition, and military equipment. The manufacturing, handling, and storage of military ordnance are, of course, hazardous at even the best of times. From time to time, an accident would occur. Flashes from explosions could be seen, followed by the sound heard all the way back to the Central Black Hills. The Army rarely had any comment or explanation. Even if the post itself was not a secret, any details about its activities were. Rumors, such as various materials being buried onsite, abound. But that is all—no details, facts, or proof, just interesting stories passed down through the decades.

Top: This was the western entrance to the contonement area.

Middle: These barracks served as housing for enlisted military personnel.

Bottom: This building had multiple functions—one of them probably was a fire station.

The extremely remote location of the Black Hills Ordnance Depot was picked for both safety and security concerns. Due to its location on an open prairie, it would have been difficult for anyone to sneak up on this post unnoticed. The same geography made the base an open book for satellite surveillance. One would have thought that security might have been compromised when the Post Hotel became famous throughout Fall River County for hosting wild parties regularly on Saturday nights.

At its peak, the population of Igloo numbered in the thousands, mostly civilian. There was a hospital, newspaper, recreation center, several movie theaters, schools, a bowling alley, and more. The Army even built a small airport. The children in neighboring Provo even went to high school at Igloo.

Provo was the nearest town to the base. A railway spur ran from the Burlington Railroad line here. This spur completely encircled the post and used its own switcher engines. These locomotives ran railcars back and forth between Provo and the post. Provo was a small community even then, so soldiers traveled the distance to Edgemont for local entertainment.

The post was closed in phases from 1965 through 1967. The Igloo High School made the state basketball playoffs during the 1965-1966 school year. Several attempts were made to convert the base for civilian use. These included feedlot construction and storage enterprises, but none succeeded. A small civilian population hung on for a short while. In 1970, Igloo was listed as having a population of ten. Since then, a local rancher bought the post. He has posted the land and is tearing buildings down and selling the scrap for salvage. Even though the land is posted, you are not trespassing as long as you stay on the county road. This is a paved road and allows

Top: One of a number of churches that served the community of Igloo.

Middle: A gas/service station located near the east gate.

Bottom: These grass-covered streets and sidewalks reveal where some of Igloo residential areas once stood.

anybody a good look at the post service area. The old processing and storage areas can easily be seen in the distance. Even though the site has been reduced by the wholesale demolishing of its buildings, there is still much to see here. The private residences are gone, but the streets and sidewalks outline where they once stood. Still visible are barracks, a church, a service station, a bowling alley, guard posts, a fire station, and much more.

Do not leave the county road because then you will be trespassing. As always, please respect private property. Igloo is marked on numerous older maps and atlases. The former residents of Igloo still have an annual reunion every third Sunday of July in Rapid City, South Dakota.

OBLIVION (Pennington)

Oblivion was created as a tourist railroad station for the original "1880 Train." Situated 4.36 miles east of Hill City, it was the turnaround point for what was then a narrow-gauge operation. There were plans to expand the tourist operation with a museum, a gift shop, and more. In 1964, the rail line converted to a standard-gauge operation and used Keystone as its turnaround point. Plans for the expansion and use of Oblivion as a rail point ceased. The train and time both passed by.

The location originally operated as a lumber camp. The Nelson sawmill processed the timber here and was serviced by a railroad. A narrow-gauge spur tied into it. It ran up Palmer Gulch and served the lumbering operations.

In the late 1950s, an elaborate narrow-gauge wye was set up. This was used to turn the tourist train back around to Hill City. It is a complex set of superimposed standard- and narrow-gauge track switches. It is a unique arrangement and is of great interest to railroad buffs. On the morning of August 18, 1957, the first official running of the tourist train, the Black Hills Central, and its turnaround were accomplished.

This was the depot at Oblivion.

Left: The first view of Oblivion from the 1880 Train.

Below: This caboose was left from the days of the narrow-gauge operation.

Oblivion has a short list of movie credits to add to its history. The location has been used for television commercials, an HBO special, and one of the sets for both the movie *Orphan Train* and a double episode of *Gunsmoke* titled "Snow Train."

Remains consist of a caboose, a railroad depot station, and the old narrow-gauge wye. There are silent telegraph poles here, but they follow the railway between Hill City and Keystone and are not just part of Oblivion. An old cabin sits back in the woods, and its roof tells me it is much older than the tourist train turnaround. The entire location is easily visible from the train.

PACTOLA LAKE VISITOR CENTER (Pennington)

This place makes for an excellent daytime stop for those in search of recreation or history. The Pactola Lake Visitor Center is located adjacent to the dam at Lake Pactola. Inside the center is a museum of both the human and natural history of the Black Hills. Free educational films for all ages are shown on a regular basis. The staff at the center is cheerful, informed, and eagerly helpful. There is no admission charged for the center or museum. There is a picnic ground, clean restrooms, and a panoramic view of the lake. Parking is plentiful and highway access easy. You should be careful of competing highway traffic when entering or exiting this parking lot.

This is all that remains of the Pactola CCC Camp. There is even less remaining of the town of Pactola. The history of both can be found nearby at the Pactola Lake Visitor Center, run by the Forest Service.

Just north of the visitor center is another highway pull-off where there is a highway historical marker and another beautiful view of the lake. Boating, fishing, and swimming are permitted at this mountain lake. Of course, you need a license to fish and a tolerance of cold water to swim. Forest Service campgrounds are nearby. On my last visit, the effects of a severe drought were showing.

An additional historical note is about the lake's location. It was built on top of the sites of three gold-rush towns. All were among the first mining camps of the Hills. First, a small portion of Silver City's original layout was submerged under the lake. Second, Elkhorn is completely under the lake. Elkhorn was a small miners' camp and railroad stop for the Black Hills and Western Railroad. It had also been called Bear Gulch. Third was the gold-rush town of Pactola, hence the lake's name. Gold was discovered here in July 1875. A few miners panned for gold and quickly set up a mining district. General George W. Crook cleared most of these men out during his 1876 expedition. He set up a camp on the site and operated his patrols from here. Within months, the miners drifted back, and the place became known as Camp Crook. A post office was established in 1877. The miners held a public meeting and changed the town's name so as not to be confused with Crook City. The town's population faded away to just a score of settlers by the early 1880s.

Another place from the past buried under the lake was a CCC Camp. The camp had been commissioned on May 18, 1933. Its dedication marker sits on the dam, which was completed in 1956. There are no remains from any of these past locations under the lake. One cabin from Pactola survived below the dam until the late 1970s or early 1980s.

Pactola Lake is on U.S. Highway 385 about eleven miles north of Hill City, South Dakota.

1880 TRAIN (Pennington)

A must-see, or must-do, in the Black Hills is the "1880 Train." This is a tourist train that runs inexpensive and scenic daytime excursions. Called the "Black Hills Central Railroad," it follows a portion of the original route of the Chicago, Burlington and Quincy Railroad. Much of the railway, steam engines, rolling stock, and company equipment have been restored to appear as a railroad operation from the turn of the last century. A trip on the Black Hills Central Railroad is fun and informative for either a historian or railroad buff. With the vintage trains and the scenic Black Hills backdrop, this is a natural subject for photographers. It also makes for a wonderful family outing.

A ride on the 1880 Train can be described in one word: "Fun!"

This is a nationally registered landmark. The railroad has an open-air museum at its Hill City terminus. It has a good number and variety of old engines and rolling stock on display. There is a ticket office and gift shop at both the Keystone and the Hill City stations. These are located in the old, rebuilt railroad depots. The rail line and its trains have been used in the production of television series, commercials, and movies. The remains of Addie Camp, Oblivion, and the Good Luck Tungsten mine are visible during the train ride.

The history of the CB&Q Railroad in the Black Hills is centered on the area's mining boom. The railroad was built to serve the area's mills, mines, and mining boomtowns. Construction started on a spur from the main Burlington line in southwestern South Dakota during the spring of 1890. This railroad intersection became the town of Edgemont, South Dakota. This line reached Deadwood on January 24, 1891.

This is the Hill City Depot. There is another in Keystone.

The 1880 Train uses the portion of track that was constructed in stages between the early 1890s and the summer of 1900. A lot of dynamite and numerous bridging trestles were used in the construction of this route. This is a standard-gauge rail operation, but many others in the Black Hills were narrow-gauge. It has up to a 6 percent grade, which is steep for a standard-gauge line. A portion of this rail line was built so that it could operate both gauges. This system, called a wye, uses a complex series of switches and superimposed tracks; it is a big attraction for railroad enthusiasts. A narrow-gauge tour train operated between Hill City and Oblivion from 1957 to 1960 using this system.

Railroads in the Black Hills, including the CB&Q, suffered frequently from devastating forest fires and flash floods. These same fires and floods have destroyed numerous ghost towns. When mining booms went bust, so did many railroads. The CB&Q route, known as the "High Line," was one of the last to operate. The last freight train into Hill City was on November 8, 1983. By this time, the Burlington Northern owned the line. The Burlington Railroad abandoned the rest of the "High Line" when it stopped operations to Custer, South Dakota, in October 1986. The abandoned railbed has since been converted into a multiuse trail known as the George S. Mickelson Trail.

The 1880 Train started excursion rides as the Black Hills Central Railroad on August 18, 1957. At this time, regular freight operations of the Burlington Northern still shared the line. Since that time, the 1880 Train has gone through changes in equipment, ownership, and route.

For about five years, the tourist train ran between Custer and Hill City. This is because a severe flash flood on Battle Creek had wiped out three miles of track. It was not until 1977 that these rail operations returned to Keystone.

Even though the engines for this railroad are old-fashioned steam locomotives, they do not burn coal, they burn oil instead. That process began in the 1920s to avoid the fire hazards the coal cinders cause when leaving the locomotive's exhaust stack. At first, bunker oil was used, but now used motor oil is burned instead.

You have a choice between open-air cars and enclosed passenger seating. The enclosed cars are a swell prize. They were originally built in 1913 in St. Louis and have been restored to their original grandeur. A historical narration is given over a speaker system during the ride.

This can be a very busy attraction during the tourist season, and reservations may be a good idea. The train operates from mid-May to early October, with full services running from June 15 through Labor Day. This attraction has its own web site: *http://1880train.com*.

Top: Patricia Cracchiola preparing to board one of the 1880 railroad's restored and historic passenger cars. Many of these cars were originally built in her hometown of St. Louis.

Bottom: This is the open-air railroad museum at Hill City.

POSTSCRIPT

ghost towns of the black hills

ou will find a number of additional sites listed in books or on websites that are not
mentioned here. The reason is simple. These sites are not Black Hills ghost towns.
These additional locations form their own subgroups. Many that are listed, such
as Okaton, South Dakota, are far outside of the Black Hills. Others, like Deadwood,
have populations in the thousands and, thus, do not qualify as ghosts.

More, like Hermosa, Edgemont, and Whitewood, South Dakota, are close to being
ghosts but are still not there. These towns have many vacant old buildings. The
locations are very historical and mere fractions of their boom sizes, but they still
do not qualify as true sleepers. Still, Hermosa, Edgemont, and Whitewood are
worth a visit. Edgemont has an attractive and historic city park that makes a nice
picnic stop. The Trails, Rails and Pioneers Museum is adjacent to the park. It is an
informative stop and is highly recommended.

Many other sites listed elsewhere simply have no remains now and, therefore ,were
not included in this book. There are other places with remains, but they have
blended into and been absorbed by the suburbs of Deadwood. They too are mostly
lost to progress and left out of this body of work.

This WWI artillery piece rests quietly in the City Park of Edgemont.

GLOSSARY

Adobe - A sun-dried brick; the mixed earth or clay of which such bricks are made.

Aerial tramway - A system for the transportation of material, such as ore or rock, in buckets suspended from pulleys or grooved wheels that run on a cable, usually stationary. A moving or traction rope is attached to the buckets and may be operated by either gravity or other power.

Alkali flat - A sterile plain, containing an excess of alkali, at the bottom of an undrained basin in an arid region.

Alkali water - Water heavy in dissolved salts or minerals. The water is unfit for human or animal consumption.

Amalgamation - The process in which gold and silver are extracted from pulverized ores by producing an amalgam, from which the mercury is later expelled.

Arrastra (or arrastre) - Apparatus for grinding and mixing ores by means of dragging around a heavy stone upon a circular bed. The arrastra is chiefly used for ores containing free gold. Amalgamation is combined with the grinding.

Assay - To test ores or minerals by chemical or blowpipe examination. Gold and silver require an additional process, called cupelling, for the purpose of separating them from the base metals.

Assay Value - The amount of the gold or silver, in ounces per ton of ore, produced by assaying any given sample.

Bar - Accumulation of gravel along the banks of a stream, which when worked by the miners for gold, is called bar diggings.

Bar mining - The mining of river bars, usually between low and high waters, although the stream is sometimes deflected, and the bar worked below water level.

Basin - A large or small depression in the surface of the land, the lowest part of which may be occupied by a lake or pond. An area or tract having certain common features throughout, particularly a tract where the strata dip from all sides toward a center.

Bedrock - The solid rock underlying auriferous gravel, sand, clay, etc. Alluvial gold rests upon this rock.

Bonanza - In miner's phrase, good luck, or a body of rich ore. A mine is in bonanza when it is profitably producing ore.

Bullion - Uncoined gold and silver; gold and silver coined but considered only with reference to its commercial value as raw material. Figuratively, solid gold or silver, hence solid worth.

Carbonates - Ores containing a considerable proportion of carbonate of lead.

Chlorination process - The process in which auriferous ores are first roasted to oxidize the base metals, then saturated with chlorine gas, and finally treated with water. This removes the soluble chloride of gold, which is subsequently precipitated and melted into bars.

Chute - A channel or shaft underground, or an inclined trough aboveground, through which ore falls or is "shot" by gravity from a higher to a lower level.

Claim - The portion of mining ground held under the Federal and local laws by one claimant or association, by virtue of one location and record; the portion of land upon a gold field to which a miner is legally entitled.

Color - The shade or tint of the earth (or rock) that indicates ore; a particle of metallic gold found in the prospector's pan after a sample of earth or crushed rock has been "panned out."

Concentrate - That which has been reduced to a state of purity or concentration by the removal of foreign, nonessential, or diluted matter.

Concentrator - An apparatus in which, by the aid of water (or air) and specific gravity, mechanical concentration of ores is performed.

Cribbing - Close timbering, as in the lining of a shaft.

Cyanide process - The extraction of gold from finely crushed ores, concentrates, and tailings using potassium cyanide in dilute solutions. The gold is dissolved by the solution and subsequently deposited upon metallic zinc or by other means.

Diggings - Applicable to all mineral deposits and mining camps; in the United States, it applies to placer mining only.

Dredge - A power-operated scoop or suction apparatus that is usually mounted on a flat-bottomed boat. It is extensively used in mining gold-bearing sand and gravel.

Drift - A horizontal passage underground. A drift follows a vein, as distinguished from a crosscut, which intersects it.

Face - The surface exposed by excavation.

Fissure vein - A cleft or crack in the rock material of the earth's crust filled with mineral matter different from the walls and precipitated therein.

Float - Pieces of ore or rock that have fallen from veins or strata or that have been separated from the parent vein or strata by weathering agencies.

Flotsam - Material that is suspended and floating. In mining terms, this is the material that makes up the riverbed and slowly floats over the bedrock sitting below it.

Flume - An inclined channel, usually of wood and often supported on a trestle, for conveying water from a distance to be utilized for power, transportation, etc., as in placer mining, logging, etc.

Flux - A substance, such as borax or alkali, that promotes the fusing of minerals or metals.

Free gold - Gold not combined with other substances.

Free-milling - Applies to ores that contain free gold or silver. It can be reduced by crushing and amalgamation without roasting or any other chemical treatment.

Galena - The most common lead mineral.

Gallows - A frame consisting of two uprights and a crosspiece for supporting a mine roof.

Gallows frame - A frame supporting a pulley, over which the hoisting rope passes to the engine.

Gold amalgam - A variety of native gold containing mercury.

Gold dust - Fine particles of gold, such as those that are obtained in placer mining.

Grubstake - Supplies furnished to a prospector on promise of a share in his discoveries. It is called such because the lender stakes or risks the grub (food), etc., so furnished.

Headframe - A structure erected over a shaft to carry the sheaves over which the cable runs for hoisting the cage. In England, it is called a gallows frame.

High-grade - Rich ore.

High grading - To steal or pilfer ore or gold, as from a mine by a miner.

Hoist - An engine for raising ore, rock, coal, etc., from a mine and for lowering and raising men and material.

Horn silver – Silver chloride.

Hydraulic mining - A method of mining in which a bank of gold-bearing earth or gravel is washed by a powerful jet of water and carried with sluices, where the gold separates from the earth by specific gravity.

Ingot - A cast bar or block of metal.

Lode - A fissure in the country-rock that is filled with mineral; a tabular deposit of valuable mineral between definite boundaries.

Long Tom - An inclined trough in which gold-bearing earth or gravel is crudely washed. It is longer than a rocker.

Low-grade - A term applied to ores relatively poor in the metal for which they are mined; lean ore.

Mill - Any establishment for reducing ores by means other than smelting.

Milling ore - A dry ore that can be amalgamated or treated by leaching and other processes. These ores are usually low-grade and free, or nearly so, from base metals.

Mother lode - The principal lode or vein passing through a district or particular section of country.

Narrow-gauge railroad - Narrowest of three widths of track used for railroads—

the others being standard- and wide-gauge. Narrow-gauge railroads are often used in the mountains.

Nugget - A lump of native gold, silver, platinum, copper, etc.

Outcrop - The rising of a stratum to the surface of the ground.

Pan - To wash earth, gravel, etc., in a pan while searching for gold.

Patent - Title in fee, obtained by patent from the United States Government when an equivalent of five hundred dollars worth of work has been done on or for each mining claim.

Pinch - The narrowing of a vein or deposit.

Pinched - Where a vein narrows, as if the walls had been squeezed in. When the walls meet, the vein is said to be "pinched out."

Placer - A place where gold is obtained by washing; an alluvial or glacial deposit, such as that of sand or gravel, containing particles of gold or other valuable mineral.

Placer claim - A mining claim, located on gravel or ground whose mineral contents are extracted by the use of water, by sluicing, by using hydraulics, etc.

Placer mining - A form of mining in which the surficial detritus is washed for gold or other valuable minerals. When pressurized water is employed to break down the gravel, the term hydraulic mining is generally employed.

Pocket - A small body of ore.

Pyrite - A hard, heavy, shiny, yellow mineral generally found in cubic crystals.

Quartz mill - A machine or establishment used for pulverizing quartz ore so that the gold and silver from the ore may be separated by chemical means; a stamp mill.

Reduction works - Works for reducing metals from their ores, as in a smelting works, cyanide plant, etc.

Reef - A lode or vein; a word introduced into mining by sailors who left their ships to participate in the rush to Ballarat and Bendigo in 1851. To them, a rock projecting above the water was a reef. The term was therefore applied to quartz outcrops on land.

Roasting and reduction process - The treatment of lead ores by roasting to form lead-oxide and subsequently reducing fusion in a shaft furnace.

Rocker - A short trough in which auriferous sands are agitated by oscillation, in water, to collect their gold.

Sawmill - A facility used to convert raw timber into lumber.

Sluice - A long, inclined trough or flume, usually found on the ground, for washing auriferous earth.

Sluice box - A wooden trough in which alluvial beds are washed for the recovery of gold or tinstone.

Smelt - To reduce metals from their ores by a process that includes fusion. In its restricted sense, smelting is confined to a single operation, as in the fusion of an iron ore in a shaft furnace, the reduction of a copper matte in a reverberatory furnace, and the extraction of a metal from sweepings in a crucible. In general, it includes the entire treatment of the material from the crude to the finished metal.

Smelter - An establishment where ores are smelted.

Soiled Dove - An old western term for female prostitute.

Stamp mill - The building or apparatus in which rock is crushed by descending pestles (stamps) that are operated by water or steampower.

Standard-gauge railroad - Middle of three widths of track for used for railroads—the others being narrow- and wide-gauge. Most railroads in the U.S. are standard-gauge.

Tailings - The worthless slime left behind after the valuable portion of the ore has been separated by dressing or concentration.

Tie town - A town where railroad ties are either milled from timber or floated downstream in large groups like cattle drives. It is usually located on a railroad line.

Unwater - To pump water from mines.

Wire silver - Native silver in the form of wire or threads.

Wye - A complex set of superimposed standard- and narrow-gauge track switches used to operate trains of two different gauged tracks on one railbed.

A partial list of terms was obtained from Albert H. Fax, through the U.S. Department of the Interior, Bureau of Mines. Bulletin 95. Washington, D.C.: Government Printing Office, 1920.

BIBLIOGRAPHY

This bibliography includes only the books that are referenced. Every possible source was used, especially maps and websites. One of the many websites I used is the copyrighted Gary B. Speck Publications site. It lists information from articles and books he has written. Interviews were conducted both in person and over the phone. Information was also confirmed or gathered from maps, pamphlets, booklets, flyers, and brochures.

Backcountry Treks. Discovery Travel Adventures. Bethesda, MD: Discovery Communications, 2000.

Baity, Dale. *Ghost Town Maps: A Guide to the Historic Towns of the Black Hills of South Dakota.* Vermillion, SD: s.n., 1990.

Florin, Lambert. *Ghost Towns of the West.* [New York]: Promontory Press, 1971.

———. *Western Ghost Towns.* Seattle: Superior Publishing Co., 1961.

Jaros, Tom, and Rick W. Mills. *All Aboard the 1880 Train.* Hill City, SD: The Black Hills Railroad, 2004.

Miller, Don. *Ghosts of the Black Hills.* Missoula, MT: Pictorial Histories Publishing Co., 1979.

Off the Beaten Path. Pleasantville, NY: Reader's Digest Association, 1987.

Parker, Watson. *Gold in the Black Hills.* Pierre, SD: South Dakota State Historical Society Press, 2003.

Parker, Watson, and Hugh K. Lambert. *Black Hills Ghost Towns.* Chicago: Swallow Press, 1974.

Patera, Alan H., John S. Gallagher, and Kenneth W. Stach. *South Dakota Post Offices.* Lake Grove, OR: The Depot, 1990.

Wallace, Robert. *The Miners.* Edited by the editors of Time-Life Books. New York: Time-Life Books, 1976.

Wild West. Discovery Travel Adventures. Bethesda, MD: Discovery Communications, 1999.

Wolle, Muriel Sibell. *The Bonanza Trail: Ghost Towns and Mining Camps of the West.* Bloomington, IN: Indiana University Press, 1953.

INDEX

This photo of the author was taken at Badlands National Park.

ABOUT THE AUTHOR

Bruce A. Raisch, ghost town hunter, historian, and photographer, has always had an appreciation and a love of history. His father was a history teacher. By age eleven, Raisch was already climbing pyramids in Mexico. This affinity for history led Raisch to the Black Hills in 1997 on his first trip to research ghost towns.

Following a family tradition of military service, he spent twenty years in the Army National Guard. He served in deployments to Honduras, Panama (twice), Kuwait, and Saudi Arabia.

Raisch has a bachelor's degree in business administration and management. Currently, he resides in St. Louis, Missouri, and is a member of the St. Louis Writers Guild.

You may learn more about the author and his books at his website: www.theghosttownhunter.com.